Human Liberty and American Democracy

Human Liberty and American Democracy

A Study in Economics, Politics, and Power

Raven Walker

iUniverse, Inc.

New York Lincoln Shanghai

Human Liberty and American Democracy
A Study in Economics, Politics, and Power

All Rights Reserved © 2004 by Raven Walker

iUniverse, Inc.

For information address:
iUniverse, Inc.
2021 Pine Lake Road, Suite 100
Lincoln, NE 68512
www.iuniverse.com

ISBN: 0-595-31821-5

Printed in the United States of America

CONTENTS

PART I

The Choice

The Choice

History has posed the question. Can a society be free? Or must most of the people be hierarchically controlled by a few, who enjoy relative liberty through position or privilege, who, by restricting or suppressing the liberty of the many, maintain that position and privilege, not by merit, but by using unequal power. Or is there any choice?

Human liberty is a body of rights, conditions, and opportunities, involving what we are free to do, or not do, which may be present in society to a greater or lesser degree. It exists only between the extremes. At one end, we have mythical anarchy, where each individual is totally free and willing to do whatever they want and can get away with. This is the panic stricken, brutish world of Hobbes. At the other end is tyranny, where all necessary power is arranged and applied to make sure that each individual's thoughts, speech, and deeds, conform to the wants, desires, and expectations of the ruler or ruling class. Power to enforce actions that favor the privileged at the clear, unwanted cost of unprivileged, however duped to accept their fates. This is the chilling, invasive world of Orwell.

The thoughtful social philosophers throughout history generally agree that only through Law can anarchy and tyranny be prevented. But not just any law. The despot can make law to reinforce and perpetuate his tyranny. For a society to prove effectively stable, free, and progressive, the Law must contain some element of justice, that is, the application of its power must be somewhat evenly distributed throughout large sections of society, if not all. The rich man's son and the poor man's son should face equal consequences for their actions. Likewise, each should succeed accordingly to their personal merits, and not according to exaggerated artificial favoritism. The Golden Rule of Liberty is the Golden Rule of all Morality. You cannot expect others to grant you what you are unwilling to grant them. Any right you claim for yourself must belong to all, or not at all. Such would be a just society, and if achieved, a free society, one where the progressive nature of human liberty expresses and effects a real future far beyond any potential found in anarchy or tyranny. Free to become what we can become. Free to fail trying, growing stronger for the try.

The power to make law is the power to make society. The answer to the question as to whether a society is to be free, or subjugated, depends on who has the right to make the law. The issue has always been, the few or the many. But law is not enough. A culture of freedom is necessary. The people need to be accustomed to the business of choices and the practice of tolerance. They need to find the risks and uncertainties of freedom to be points of departure for adventure and discovery, instead of occasions of fear and avoidance. They must believe that the prospect of an unknown personal destiny promises a far better future than a life already worked out in detail from cradle to grave.

But to establish and maintain the conditions of liberty through law, one must break the power of the few who would use their considerable power to usurp the law to suppress liberty in the many to their exclusive benefit. Human liberty must always free itself from bondage. This takes power, overmatching power, which at this deepest level of social construction can only be found in the Will of the People, an exceedingly difficult and rare consensus. At this point, one could ask whether liberty is worth the contentions, revolutions, and bother its establishment invariably requires. If there are no gains or worth in free society above what can be found in the beehive systems of tyranny, why go to all the pain and effort? Is the goal of liberty another false god?

History provides one answer. Wherever, despite enormous and baffling imperfections, events occur, or actions are taken, in either the political or economic realms, opening up society to the real experience in the conditions of liberty, new energies are released in the nation, expressing themselves as golden ages, wanderlusts, enlightenments, and ages of invention and progress. Tyranny is often successful in arranging power to its satisfaction, but such societies become rigid, repetitive, and unadaptive. They fall hard like overdeveloped dinosaurs.

Psychology provides another answer. In a society where individual thought, speech, manner, and conduct is prescribed in detail, and pervasively enforced with ant hill efficiency, one learns to conform one's thought, speech, manner, and conduct by rote. To follow the rule and conform correctly, this is the end to be achieved. The more organized our behavior is by rote learning, the more like the rat in the Skinner box we become. We become rigid, fixed, inflexible, and unadaptive. To function in a culture of freedom, one must largely employ process learning. We proceed toward goals, objectives, and expected outcomes, by considering means and judging their worth. In a free society, one is free to learn, free to try, free to fail. A society fostering process learning evolves, adapts, innovates and progresses.

To illustrate the difference between the two modes of behavior, a problem in manners can be considered, how to be polite to another person? In rote behavior, one identifies and trains oneself in the rule for conduct, some specific prescription in gesture and manner, and displays it upon the appropriate occasions correctly. To fulfill the prescription is to be polite. In process behavior, one identifies the desired outcome, to set the other at ease and induce welcome feelings, and while rules, forms, and customs are not ignored, they are not found sufficient if the outcome is not met. Process conduct keeps its eye on the outcome and is free to vary means to better achieve that end.

The conditions of human liberty are fertile ground. Only in a culture of freedom do the struggles of human existence bear fruit worth all the suffering.

The Great American Experiment

The myth is that the American Revolution inaugurated an unprecedented experiment in liberty. The consensus of the European ruling classes was that it would not long endure. The historical record tells another story. The real miracle is that American Democracy actually developed against such odds.

The American Revolution was no experiment or revolution at all, let alone one in liberty or democracy. A revolution occurs when significant and discontinuous changes occur in cultural institutions, social, political, and economic. For most of the upper crust rebel leaders, for example, the signers of the Declaration of Independence, the conflict was about the right to put their own name on the franchise marquis instead of the name of some dead king buried in England. A rebellion only, a war for independence and political sovereignty, with no planned changes in how things were to be run at home. Much of the content of the United States Constitution was designed to make sure that the power to control things to their aristocratic advantage was firmly placed and held by the existing, European, feudal ruling class, albeit native this time around.

The United States Constitution, while providing for a survivable national government, a federal government uniting several, separate states, is essentially a deliberate, pre-emptive counter-revolutionary document. It was written by perhaps the 55 wealthiest men in America, who were each more than dispassionately interested in securing the extremely favorable position the expulsion of British authority had placed them in. They designed a government to sanctify and protect this happy status quo forever. They expected to keep their property and power intact and growing, damn the torpedoes. What else would an incipient, wannabe aristocracy do but fix the technical arrangements of government to keep and safeguard their privileged position in society, that is, maintain a hierarchy of social classes, a pyramid of privilege, wealth, and power, instead of a society of individuals and types working off a level landscape. Many of the Founding Fathers wanted, and expected, all the power and wealth enjoyed by their contemporary ruling classes of the Great European Nation States. Mere changes in form, but no changes in substance. Create and preserve the same hierarchical society so profitable to the few at the top of the pyramid.

The American ruling class rebels benefited three ways from the successful repulsion of British sovereignty and power. First, the governmental instruments of power were left in their hands. Second, perhaps up to a third of America's wealth fell into their laps, the spoils of war resulting from the confiscations, abandonments, and dispossessions of the American Loyalists, those members of the ruling class content with British domination. This was a massive re-distribution and concentration of wealth in the hands of a few, not unlike the shifts in wealth accomplished during the Reformation, when the existing nobility expropriated ecclesiastical properties in the name of nationalism. Third, the rebelling aristocracy discovered the joys of war profiteering and holding government debts accruing interest. The new national government secured all these claims, as well as their military service claims as officers in the Continental Army amounting to half pay for life. This when the most frequent cause of common rank veterans leaving the War was the prolonged absence of any pay whatsoever. No wonder, life, liberty, and the pursuit of happiness became life, liberty, and property.

With all this new wealth and power, the rebel aristocrats were able to subject the common people, the many, to the exertions of a tyranny far more effective than what the British Empire had been able to project across a two month ocean. By the mid 1780's, the stage for a real revolution was set. In 1786, the populace of the New England countryside rebelled against the concerted, well organized injustice driving them into serfdom. The conflagration would be called Shay's Rebellion, and would spread from Western Massachusetts, to Connecticut, Rhode Island, and Vermont. These were the same people who stood up at

Lexington and Concord twenty years before and faced the best of British military power at Bunker Hill.

Massachusetts, the so called cradle of liberty, led the repression of the conservative reaction. Of all States, only patricians of Massachusetts had the nerve to actually raise the property qualification for suffrage, thus blatantly tightening their hierarchical control. The common people, who had born heavy sacrifices during the War for Independence, found themselves strapped down like cattle. If they rented, they faced expropriating levies. If they bought, they faced interest laden payments and sudden foreclosure. If they held free, they faced a dozens petty taxes from county, town, courts and the state, to be paid in hard coin, going to support the sheriffs, constables, judges, bailiffs, and assessors who evicted them from their tenancies, imprisoned them for debt, and foreclosed on their properties, selling all they possessed in low bid, fast cash auctions. If you held a debt and could not pay on call, the government apparatus your taxes supported enforced the laws of contract, and cashed you in, sickbed and all.

These conditions of unjust society went on for years before the common man rebelled in collective protest. They organized themselves into minute men like milita units by the thousands, drilled and behaved in a military manner, and either paraded or showed up in mass at the opening day of the local or regional General Court, demanding it postpone its proceedings. In other words, stopping the business of repression and democratically registering a just grievance.

Shay's Rebellion was essentially a peaceful protest, much like the Bonus March of the American veterans of World War I in 1931 Washington. When the Confederation Army showed up and hung a dozen ringleaders, it played out, just as the Bonus Marchers fled town after MacArthur burned them out. The historical parallel with the Peasant's Revolt in Reformation Germany in 1530 is instructive because of the long running build up of injustice present at that time in Europe. When the newly enriched princes and their lieges merely continued the existing social regime with more vigor, the serfs and peasants, filled with the zeal and confidence of religious liberation, rose up by the hundreds of thousands, destroying unprotected castles and burning feudal deeds by the bonfire. The nobility and their armed retainers withdrew into their moatted fortresses, and waited for the peasants to go home to bring in the harvest. Then they descended in their might and hung, burned, or crucified the ringleaders and anyone else handy by the tens of thousands, while the Emperor and Martin Luther looked on with approval.

Strange how the common folk never seem to adapt to the inferior status the conservative elite consider their natural condition.

In Massachusetts, the nobility withdrew into their city money credit system. They starved the countryside by refusing to issue paper money, requiring all payments to be made in specie, all the specie already well horded in Boston. When the national military power restored order, they hurried to Philadelphia to see that a stronger national government was formed, one that would sanctify and uphold their practices, save their property, and prevent any more popular uprisings from occurring again and spreading farther. The Founding Fathers went to Philadelphia to protect themselves from democracy, not foster it. Their victims, too, were on the move. They fled West to escape the brutal repression and abuse, the tyranny, of the caste ridden seaboard.

The origins, then, of the American Democratic Spirit are a good deal more obscure than one would imagine. There is the intellectual tradition that is traced through John Locke, and is so ably expressed in the Declaration of Independence. The intelligentsia were also aware of Montesquiex and Rosseau, and having classical educations, were knowledgeable of the throes and pangs of Athenian Democracy. This was also the time of the Scottish Enlightenment, with its unity of science and the humanities to promote a cultured society, as well as its belief in the progressive nature of a just society. Adam Smith was a special favorite.

This is a great tradition, and represents today the bulwark behind any modern democratic experiment. But one must remember that only a few early Americans were literate, and even fewer, well educated. The intellectual classes do not carry through revolutions. Unless the many are moved, great ideas are largely wishful thinking.

Further, Locke's justification for revolution was never intended to support a popular democratic movement. In fact, when Locke drafted constitutions for the Carolinas in the 1660's, he setup a feudal aristocracy complete with barons holdings vast estates. The whole aim of his political arguments was to provide the rising business class with a rationale for muscling in on the political power being held exclusively by an aged, landed aristocracy. Greece, Rome, and the Italian Renaissance, even the Cromwell dictatorship, provide numerous examples of this ruling class reorganization. There were always Levelers around, but they were discredited as too radical, and too foolish to be seriously considered. In other words, Locke argued for a revolution in the composition of the ruling class, but there was no idea of disturbing the traditional power of the ruling elite once reconstituted. In fact, for many early Americans, rebels and tories alike, this was all that the trouble was about. One nascent, native ruling class fighting to establish independence from a mothering, yet foreign ruling class. The stakes were, which few were to rule and exploit the many.

So what, then, are the primal sources of American Democracy. First, there is the matter of the Scots. In the 1700's, unleashed by their own expansion of liberty through the Act of Union and their indigenous Enlightenment, the Scots migrated to America in disproportionately large numbers, usually in small groups, often as individuals, and dispersed themselves broadly throughout the population, from city to frontier. They brought with them several ingrained characteristics. Though they had had to suffer and overthrow the tyranny of John Knox's theocracy, they had seen the power and competence of democracy at work in religion. There was little doubt that the power of the Kirk rested upon the Will of the People despair as one might its intolerance. The extension of the Democratic Spirit to the political and economic realms seemed obvious and trustworthy.

The migrating Scots were also the beneficiaries of the first national, universal public education system in the Western World, established and enforced by the Kirk. The Scots arriving on American shores could read, write, and add, and many were educated well beyond basic literacy. They were instant economic assets in the New World. Many black Americans bear Scottish last names because Scots made ideal plantation overseers. These people had cut their teeth in an environment rich in independent national identity, religious democracy, personal liberty, and possessed a thorough going belief that political and economic freedom was the source of social well being, progress, and individual success. But if the Scots were well positioned to serve as the fuses and sparks of democratic movement, where did the explosive mass come from?

The answer lies in the nature of the New World conditions. For many generations, the American frontier was lined up on the river banks and sea shores. The numbers in the first wave groups were small, even band size. Conditions were primitive and primal. They were surrounded by aboriginal tribes, with whom they first cooperated, and then completely destroyed. To survive, the first invading Americans had to revert to Tribalism, and did so in a very ugly way. They were small groups of humans who had to bond together politically, and share economically, in order to remain a coherent, effective group capable of fending off starvation, misery, and annihilation. On the seaboard, where the Old World arrived at the harbor close at hand, the tribal conditions of the New World were quickly converted into old school, hierarchical societies. The "civilized" portion of the colonies were miniature clones of the Mother Country's thousand year old feudal arrangement of political power and economic wealth, a social order based upon the military conquest and subjugation of one population by another population less numerous. The extreme concentrations of power and wealth, with its attendant significant curtailment of the liberties and rights of many others, are justified as spoils of war, and are maintained through unequal power. Feudalism, an all societies based upon its paradigm, is a form of institutionalized racketeering.

But the farther one got from the harbor, the larger the New World became. The further West you went, the more intense the primitive conditions compelling tribal societal cooperation became. The motives were numerous. Some came for the lure of the undiscovered New World, some for the lure of land to own and farm, an independent livelihood. To fulfill this dream, one had to go West. All the good Eastern land was in the hands of the aristocracy. Some were indentured servants, having worked off their bonds. Some were thugs, and others penniless with no where else to go. Many had felt the lash of the ruling class's power, as Andrew Jackson did as boy, slashed with a saber for refusing to spit polish a British officer's boots. But origins or motives meant little if you failed the conditions. The American frontier killed off as many whites as it did the peoples of the native tribes. If you survived, that was origin enough. If you succeeded, you were an entirely new kind of contemporary human being, the myth of the original American, the self reliant, independent, masterful individual, born of the frontier and beholden to no one.

Put another way, the surviving frontier cultures experienced the tribal distributions of political and economic power, where all is open to public purview and address. Where if the chief slays the weakest member of the tribe, he is driven out, or where the wealthiest must share most of his largess before being granted status. Where the distribution of personal rights and collective wealth are normatively distributed. Otherwise the tribe disintegrates and fails to survive except as splintered bands and individuals. By the time of the American Revolutions, the invading European peoples had had 150 years of living in the tribal condition of society, and the practices of liberty that such experience favors. Since much of the comfortably living seaboard opposed or were indifferent to the Revolution, the masses that carried out the Revolution were tribal culture creations. They were about as willing to compromise their liberty as were the Sioux.

But even if the sense of liberty and democratic sentiment are well spread among the many, and highly charged, the people still need a voice and a leader. That man was to be Thomas Jefferson, why the first American Democratic Revolution is properly called the Jefferson Democracy.

Natural and Unnatural Distributions

Everyone concedes that Nature bestows her gifts of ability and fortune unequally. Ability is born of nature and experience. Fortune is born of circumstance and luck. Some people are indeed lazy, while others are obsessively industrious. Some are smart and others dumb. Some people are born to privilege and well provisioned environments. Some are born in degraded ghettos and chaos. But if the physical trait or personal attribute has origins in natural causes, then the inequality is almost always distributed in the shape of the normal curve, sometimes known as the bell curve. The whole science of psychometrics and inferential statistics relies upon this fact. The normal probability distribution is Nature's paradigm of inequality. Correspondingly, highly skewed distributions are prima facie evidence that some additional cause, either as force or artifice, is operating to create the abnormal, unnatural distribution.

Human liberty depends on two foundations, one political and the other economic. These aspects are both separable and inseparable. While we can clearly and intelligibly discuss each realm in its own right, neither aspect of human society has ever occurred in isolation, or without considerable impact on the other. Any program of policy and law for affecting the shape and arrangement of one realm, without taking the conditions of the other into careful account, is either fraudulent or a waste of time.

In the political realm, the matter to be distributed throughout the nation are rights, protections, obligations, suffrage, and voice. Democratic Law, being based upon the principle that all citizens are equal before the law, prescribes an equal and even distribution of political rights, a straight line if you will. The religious contention that all humans are equal before God is consistent with this principle. But political rights have an intangible character, and power can never be wholly eliminated. Consequently, in effective terms, most democratic societies will have tilted, or slanted distributions. Someone well to do and well connected will likely fare better before the power of the law than someone poor and isolated. When the law itself prescribes or reinforces unequal preference, the distribution skews unnaturally. This is the case under slavery and feudalism, even Hammurabi's Code, where the noble born could get off with fines while the common man had his nose cut off. Clearly in such cases, human liberty is severely curtailed.

In the economic realm, the matter distributed constitutes the material standard of living, the wealth of the nation or state. In nomadic and early agrarian tribal societies, the economic distribution was normative. The fact of personal public address and inspection, and the virtue of reciprocity, both work to pile the collective wealth in the middle. But the normally shaped, natural inequality also stands to reason. A real person's productive capacity, in any sense whatsoever, faces significant psychological and physical limits. Each person has a specific modicum of physical and mental ability and has the same 24 hour day in which to apply that ability in economically productive ways. Let us say that the sole product of economic activity needed is the adobe brick. Then further allow the imaginary condition that all persons can report to a workstation that is organized and supplied in such a way that the only thing determining each person's output of adobe bricks are the ability factors. Let both strength and smarts operate in favor of those who possess such gifts. If each person retains the product of their labor, the wealth produced will be normally distributed. But if a few, at the end of the day, can claim all or most of the product of others as their own, leaving those others bereft, the distribution of wealth will be skewed, a maldistribution in fact.

This is the pyramid structure of society, a more permanent, power based version of the pyramid schemes of the con artist. But such expropriation of economic product taken against the will of the producer can only be achieved through the leverage of unequal, overwhelming power. Distortions in the natural distributions of society are caused by unnatural leveraging power, however wielded.

The actual shape of the economic and political distributions of a society, and the discrepancy between that shape and the normal shape of the natural distributions, measures the presence or absence of the conditions of human liberty in that society. How free is a society? Examine its political and economic distributions between the few and the many.

The curious question is, if wealth began naturally distributed, how did the few manage to create skewed distributions grossly in their favor, to the detriment of the many. The answer is power, whether exercised through custom, conquest, law, and once appropriated, through wealth. How else can the few subdue the many?

Jefferson and Hamilton

When the sacred founding fathers met in Philadelphia in 1787, they usurped the power of government making. They well understood that the power to make constitutional law was the power to make society. For most this was the business of insuring the status quo prevailed indefinitely, but when you open everything up and start from the beginning, anything becomes possible and other ideas come into play. From the beginning, history's two great theories of society, that of the free society and that of the hierarchical society, came into conflict. Do the many rule? Is the state a nation of people? Or do only a few and their servants, rule? Is the state and its government only a vehicle for administering the power of a self preserving aristocracy?

The guiding geniuses behind each drive to power were Thomas Jefferson and Alexander Hamilton. Jefferson and the Virginia School of Democracy chose the people and the free society. Hamilton and the Federalists chose the privileged and hierarchical society. The House of America has been deeply divided from the start. The Civil War only cleared the table of the sin of slavery. The Civil Rights Movement a hundred years later only reset the stage. A house divided still cannot stand. The American Experiment in Liberty is still an open question. It has not yet succeeded. Are we a nation of people? Or do the few, holding the power of state, get to do what they will to the many?

Both men had high, local social standing, Jefferson in Virginia, and Hamilton in New York. Both had made national names for themselves, Jefferson by writing the Declaration of Independence in 1776, and Hamilton by storming the last redoubt at Yorktown in 1781. Hamilton had the backing of many of the privileged few, and General Washington's blessing. Jefferson had to stand alone and endure while his rival carried the day and most of the new national government his way. Jefferson's only advantage might have been the belief, even faith, that social justice and democratic liberty really do align with human nature and the natural conditions of a healthy society, and have a life of their own that cannot be simply legislated away.

The irksome nature of Jefferson's ideas earned him the Ambassadorship to France during the political mayhem and social turbulence of Confederation America. He was not recalled until after the Constitutional Convention closed. Hamilton consolidated his northern power and brilliantly blended his views with Jefferson's protégé, James Madison, in the Federalist Papers, the intellectual justification for the formation of a stronger national government, a federal government of unified states, instead of a loose confederation of sovereign, petty nations. The fundamental, unresolved differences thus papered over, a compromised, ratifiable document emerged. Except that Jefferson's approval was necessary to carry the southern bloc, and the document itself said nothing whatsoever about individual liberty.

Power

Power is the ability to influence, shape, or control human events, namely the life, liberty, and actions of others, indeed, to determine the course of their living. Power can both compel or proscribe. In form of delivery, power can be exerted physically or psychologically, or as is usually the case, both in combination. By examining intents and effects, the application of power can be judged positive or negative, depending, for example, on whether the agency exerting the power does so in the interests of the person subjected to the power and not their own, and on whether the power inflicted is against the will of the person targeted or with their consent. One can drown a man or pull him from the water. The operation of power can be positive. It can lead, inspire, teach, and instill cooperation. This is true leadership, where the people follow of their own free will and not because they will be punished if they do not. But power can also simply maim and destroy, psychologically and physically. Without just cause, which is often the case, this is tyranny, power applied to keep people down, not build them up.

The medium of negative power is pain, fear of injury, or loss of life, to one's self or loved ones, or property loss, by destruction or confiscation, and otherwise all the bad things we can threaten or do unto each other. The looks and outcomes of negative power can be direct or indirect. One can experience incarceration, coerced conformity, or a direct denial of opportunity in favor of privilege. Or one can perform as a well conditioned, modern, middle class indentured servant, or as a regressed, dumbed down, bread and circuses groupie.

But many cases are not so simple. One can destroy a person by giving them what they think they want, or help a person even though pain is caused. Withholding positive applications of power can also be negative power, while negative applications can sometimes bring positive results. You can spank a child once, and get their attention, or fail to reprimand and insure they become even more reckless and undisciplined. You can deprive and persecute a group, and while you may succeed in breaking them down, you may also make them stronger and more dangerous. Power and its application is an extremely difficult and complex matter, yet it occurs a million times a day in hundreds of different ways in a single locale. One of the basic facts of human existence is that we all have power, sometimes great, sometimes small, over each other. And it affects the course of our lives, and of others, dramatically. We impose on each other all the time.

Power can be applied by an individual toward another individual or toward a group. It can also be exercised by a group on an individual or on another group. We can beat a person with our fists or we can give them CPR. We can spellbind a cult or we can lead a militia in defense of the our loved ones. We can lynch a vagrant or manage a worthy social reform. When power is invested in government through law, police power, and military force, it can be brought to bear on individuals or groups of individuals, and as the only valid group in democracy is the people, the All, no group favored among others, the conflict between power and liberty can only be resolved at the individual level. In a just society, there are no many or few, only one and all. Why else is the Golden Rule stated in individual terms?

What makes the analysis of power perplexing is that purposes and means are equally important, and they are often crossed. To evaluate purposes, we must consider whose interests are served, who benefits. To evaluate means, we must consider whose rights are at stake. Power cannot be eliminated, nor is such desirable, but its applications can be judged as rightful or wrongful. The challenge is to arrange such a control over power as to insure social justice.

Straight up power against power, without constraint, is war or anarchy. The only cultural institutions that a society has to even begin to control power are law and morality. As these can vary significantly in content and method, law and morality can both free a nation, or subjugate the many to the few. Absent the limits and guidance of a democractic theory of social justice, based upon the idea that all people possess, inalienably, certain equal rights, and are equally worthy before God and Man, law and conventional morality can be used to support, promote, and reinforce concentrations of unequal and highly skewed power, reaping the ample benefits of its service for those few possessing and using that power to their advantage and favor. Law and customary morality can quash human liberty or unleash it. There are only two choices, two directions. Toward the rigid pyramid structure of artificially enforced hierarchy, or the leveling of fully liberated democracy.

Government is only an instrument of power, and can be used variously. There are no inherently just forms of government, only just applications of power.

Government and Power

Governance evolved naturally in social animals. The pack and the pride act, adapt, and survive as a whole, yet the individuals within enjoy considerable freedom to be themselves, and broadly benefit, or suffer, with the success or failure of the group as a whole. Effective governance produces the cooperative advantage of the group over the individual, where individuals within fare better than individuals without.

Materially primitive human societies, perhaps the first 100,000 years of the species' history, organized themselves so well with respect to their demands of material sufficiency given the resources available in their environments that they were able to spend only five hours a day, on the average, on survival related work. The rest they could spend in visiting other camps of brethren, exploring, dancing, sleeping, story telling, and playing. Or nurse a grudge if they were having a bad day. In the centuries of our turn upon evolution's stage, humans have spent as much time as they could in the actual activities of happiness, maybe half. Quite often surviving aborigines of the species feel sorry for civilized, modern man, so obsessed by the rat raced pursuit of happiness through material acquisition that burnout recuperations are necessary on a daily basis. When is there time to be happy? Can that be free?

Humans are the quintessential social animal, and the conditions under which they have survived as a species much more resemble the pack and the pride than the troupes of apes and monkey flocks popular culture mocks as our primitive beginnings. Humans are highly disposed to cooperative behavior. Put any two together, and shortly they function as a team. Humans bond to others as deeply as the wolf or lion bonds. We survived on the savannah because we became tightly knit, highly efficient, bands of predators. When we turned agrarian, when we domesticated our prey and raised our pickings as crops, we brought this intense social disposition with us. The tribe is the human version of the pack and the pride. We share much in common with our animal totems, but have succeeded this much more. Compared to the relentless pursuit of food required of the rest of the Animal Kingdom, humans can enjoy real leisure. We can spent more time in the pursuits of happiness then in the work required to sustain a comfortable enough living, even if we choose not to. There are some attractive features to early human social existence worth setting as a modern goal.

But the liberty and justice enjoyed by kith and kin does not automatically extend to strangers. Strangers are from the outside the tribal society, and are either a menace, an economic resource, a grisly evening of entertainment, or sometimes, a new member of the tribe. This problem of the uncertain prospects and purposes of strangers, and how to deal with them, confounds the problem of justice and governance for social organization where the scale is much larger than that of the comforting tribe. How are we to get along with the others, when most of them are strangers? What governing arrangements, what cultural mores, are needed to get the larger whole to behave like a tribe? Some arrangement of government?

The political concept of democracy is usually confused with the usage of the word, "democracy", to describe a certain kind and set of technical arrangements in governance, as "republic" and "monarchy" describe other distinctive technical arrangements. The technical arrangements of governance are largely neutral. Considerable tyranny was exercised through the Athenian democratic structure of government. A few despots have proved as benevolent as the fabled philosopher kings. And any and all technical arrangements of government have proven capable of corruption, which has been practiced in countless different ways. There are no fail safe technical arrangements, for liberty or tyranny. The just and the unjust alike are overthrown, by conquest or revolution. Government is always subject to those welding the power, the people or the few. When the power shifts, the same governmental arrangements can be used to accomplish new, different ends.

The fundamental problem of human society, of how to cross the threshold to cooperative and well governed systems of social organization significantly larger than the tribal scale of organization, is where western political philosophy traditionally begins its ruminations, the primal state of nature where individuals see that there are remarkable benefits to all to be gained by shedding themselves of power and rights, and investing those given up to a government. The government then in operation provides the order, stability, and conflict resolution, that is beneficial to all those divesting themselves in making the social contract. The celebrated rationale for the state of nature social contract is that the individuals so conjoining themselves perceive that the survival of each as only individuals is vastly inferior to their existence as individuals within the cooperatively governed group. Less noted by western political philosophers is the presumption that all those involved must believe that their freely made contribution is equal to all others, and that the benefits to be gained through the social contract be distributed in like manner. Nothing else would be rational, though through the application of unequal power, possible.

The government so instituted becomes a focused instrument for making and enforcing law, presumably in line with the concept of justice embodied in the social contract. But such a concentration of power can be commandeered to favor the few as well as to promote the general welfare. It can be used to suppress liberty as well as release it. According to Locke's theory of revolution, when the government's actions become manifestly unjust, when it grossly violates the implied social contract, the people under its governance have the right to overthrow that government and constitute a new one, and are justified if they do so. Whatever the merits of the complaints and grievances put forward by the American colonies to prove injustice, their justification of their revolt and rebellion was pure Locke. They wanted a new deal, on better terms for themselves.

But once a specific government is overthrown, it must be reconstituted. At that moment, the nation is remarkably free to shape its future. In devising the new constitutional basis of society, the nation has considerable latitude in how it chooses to define itself, with significant differences possible in the nature of the society so defined. The final form the reconstructed government takes depends largely on how those who are usurping the power to make constitutional law perceive the sore spots that motivated the revolutionary action. It also depends on whose interests they are really representing when they make the law the creates the government that will rule the nation. The temptation is is to save privilege wherever privilege exists.

This issue, how to constitute a new national government, is at the heart of the schism between Jefferson and Hamilton. Was the War of Independence simply an internecine feud between factions within the ruling class, that is merely a rebellion of a few against a few. Or was it the prelude to true revolution and the chance expand human liberty? Would the new American government serve a nation of people, a democracy, or serve a state of special interests, an aristocracy? How you arrange the power of government, however, depends on one's theory of society, of what is possible, just, or necessary. Hamilton believed that a skewed, hierarchical structure was necessary for society to function, and that the interest of the ruling few were the interests of the state. What was good for them was good for the nation. Jefferson believed that democracy was possible and would flourish. That by granting the full measure of human liberty to all, the many become all, and the nation prospers in peace and good health.

At first, Hamilton and his ilk were in favor of strong government. They assumed they would be in control. The parties in power, and assured to stay in power, want government as strong as necessary to accomplish their interests. This is the idea behind Louis the XIVth and the divine right of kings. Jefferson and his libertarians, on the other hand, anticipated this strategy of the ruling elite, and sought to hamstring the wannabe ruling class by making government too weak to carry out their designs. But once both the Jeffersonian and Jacksonian Democracies proved capable of welding significant power over a comprehensive set of democratic objectives, through a supposedly small, weak, and limited government, the positions on strong or weak government shifted. A democracy would still have government small and limited, but keep it strong enough to register the popular will, strong enough to blunt and break the power of any emerging aristocracy, as well as strong enough to protect and promote liberty and democratic justice, that is, preserve and sustain a free society.

The conservative reaction was to insightfully switch in favor of weak government, one too feeble to project democratic power on behalf of the all. One too hobbled to attack their castles of private concentrations of wealth or the power that wealth assures. This flip flop on attitudes toward strong or weak government underscores the essentially ambivalent nature of the technical arrangements of governance. To drive the point home, consider the case of direct monetary involvement in capital industry by government action. If done for the general welfare, the many, this conduct is popularly called socialism. If done to preserve the property and interests of the business community, especially as corporations, this conduct is properly called fascism. The great issue in political philosophy is not in devising better forms of government, but in deciding which theory of society is right, the will and interests of the people, the free society devoted to liberty, or the will and interests of the few, the hierarchical society devoted to privilege.

Hamilton's Vision of the Modern Ruling Class

Let us first hear it in their own words. First from Hamilton himself.

"No society can succeed which does not unite the interest and credit of rich individuals with those of the state."

"All communities divide themselves into the few and the many. The first are rich and well born, the other the mass of the people. The people are turbulent and changing; they seldom judge or determine right."

"Give, therefore, to the first class a distinct, permanent share in the government. They will check the unsteadiness of the second, and as they cannot receive any advantage by change, they therefore will ever maintain good government."

In other words, wealth, good sense, righteousness, and right to rule, all go together and the best of all possible worlds appears. But notice the anti-progress position. The more things stay the way they are, the better they are.

Hamilton's self serving foolishness is touching. The masterpiece of idiocy the well matured aristocracies of Europe concocted in World War I suggests that the many would be hard pressed to do worse. But this is what he believed. The views of many of his kind is even more discouraging. Hear first from Chancellor Kent of Harvard, then from the Federalist's mouthpiece, the *American Quarterly Review*.

"The notion that every man that works a day on the road, or serves an idle hour in the militia, is entitled as of right to an equal participation in the whole power of government, is most unreasonable, and has no foundation in justice."

"The lowest orders of society ordinarily mean the poorest, and the highest, the richest. Sensual excess, want of intelligence, and moral debasement, distinguish the former, and knowledge, intellectual superiority, and refined social and domestic affections, the latter."

The species it seems is not a species at all, merely an imposition of one species over an inferior one, a domestication of the many if you will. There are a few angels, saints and heroes, on the one hand, and a lot of pigs, sheep, and mules on the other, desperately needing the control and discipline the brilliant few impose. It is a characteristic wickedness of the reactionary element in society to successfully conspire to hold many in low and vulgar conditions, and when such conditions have worked their degrading effects upon their victims, observe how obviously mean, vile, and inferior the many are. This is like forcing a man to live in a swamp, then telling him he deserves it because he smells like he lives in a swamp. Nowadays, the reactionary set have learned to better disguise their beliefs and purposes with words like "national security" and "compassion", as if compassion ever justified slavery.

To Hamilton and the Federalists, the American Revolution was strictly a squabble of political independence between two ruling classes. The idea that a deeper social and political revolution was in play was considered dangerous folly. The guillotine madness of the French Revolution proved this to them. The idea that the excesses of Paris were the result of a thousand years of ugly mistreatment would never occur to them. When the newly independent aristocracy looked around for a model of national governance, they could find nothing better than the British system. They would have replicated it lock, stock and barrel if they could have.

But it had been the resistance of the many, the revolutionary masses, that made the British military conquest impossible in the long run. And these many were still active and bitterly resentful of anything that smacked of the British privileged class system. In fact, during the Confederation years, all the states repealed the laws of entail and primogeniture by which the estates supporting a landed aristocracy were preserved, thus perpetuating that kind of privileged class. Indeed, the specific motivation behind these legislative acts was to prevent any land based aristocracy from ever developing in America. Benedict Arnold was considered a traitor, but he was living in England, the way the Hamiltonians dreamed of, off the comfortable, secure largess of others bound to a landed estate.

The leveling popular sentiments presented the Federalists with a problem. How to subdue the American Common after bleeding it to win the right to rule the common many like British Lords. The goals for their program were clear. To deliberately concentrate wealth and political power in the the hands of a few. To identify the national interest with the interests of the party of concentrated power. And to restrict suffrage, and use the government to safeguard the property of a permanent ruling class so that the many who were left out could not threaten the few. But by what means if landed estates were not possible?

It was Hamilton's genius to graft the pyramid structure of feudalism onto nascent industrial capitalism, and his blending of government and corporate business presages Italian fascism. If the aristocracy, the privileged class possessed of concentrated property and power, could not base itself on land, than why not base itself on capital, money? If sinecures drawn from the economic product of a landed estate and its attached labor were unavailable or unstable, why not use the national debt and its interest payments to secure the same ample cash flows necessary and sufficient to support their leisure? The privileged ruling class would then own the government, just as the old feudal lords owned all the land of the nation. Instead of a landed aristocracy, a new, moneyed aristocracy, a kind of feudal capitalism preserving the once power of conquest in land and projecting it into the new world of wealth.

To concentrate wealth and power, one must support and preserve capital. To achieve this end, establish a charter based banking system, using the political power of the national and state legislatures to create monopoly conditions, but keep the ownership in private hands. With a little finesse, the legislators and the corporate directors end up eating at the same tables, and their sons and daughters intermarry.

With control of banking,comes control of the money supply, of credit, bank notes, mortgages, and interest. And if government can sanction financial corporate monopolies, why not also other industrial, construction, or commercial enterprises? But here the concept of free trade interferes. Foreign competition, already well advanced into large scale capital industries, can threaten the success of the early stage, high cost, native corporations. So the tariff is necessary, even if this costs the many the choice of cheaper and more plentiful goods. After all, the interests of the nation are the interests of its capital holders, not its people. So the tariff too became part of Hamilton's American System.

The actual achievements of the Federalists in service of their program are as follows. The creation of a large national debt by taking over all the debts of the states and adding that to the debts of the Continental Congresses. Establishing through Congress, a privately held Bank of the United States, associated with similarly chartered state banks. Using the power of legislative corporate chartering to create additional, special corporations, also possessing monopoly conditions. Electing as President and successor to Washington, one of their own, John Adams. Winning the legal status of person for the corporation by John Marshall's judicial fiat. Passing a comprehensive tariff bill. And the United States Constitution minus the Bill of Rights.

They also resisted the extension of suffrage, State's Rights, free trade, competition, and any interference by government in business and finance, even though it was through the instrument and sanction of government that they enjoyed and preserved their position of privilege in this new world of feudal capitalism.

Jefferson's Vision of a Free Society

Jefferson was the American Ambassador to France during the Constitutional Convention, and though key elements in his political philosophy were directly incorporated into the document, those of divided, counter balancing government and State's Rights, the absence of specifically stated guarantees of individual freedom was unacceptable. If you cannot protect the individual, you cannot protect the many. So upon his return, Jefferson rallied the South and won the first ten amendments, The Bill of Rights, as the price of ratification.

Jefferson first served the new national government as Secretary of State in Washington's unity cabinet. But when it became clear that Hamilton's political philosophy was dominating administration policy, he resigned and formed an opposition party, the democracy party. From the beginning, it was to be the party of the many, and its goal was simple, at least in abstract terms. To expand human liberty as broadly as possible, protect it, and entrench it. This meant that any concentration of power, either through wealth, privilege, or even the government itself, must be prevented. The practical objective then became the extension of suffrage. In Jefferson's time, this meant lowering the dollar amount of the property holding qualification for voting rights, always bringing in more of the many, and resisting attempts to raise the purchase price of voting, the poll tax, thereby turning the citizen franchise into an obedient, manageable voting caste. It would take another two hundred years to reach universal suffrage, but the democratic principle and drive toward an equal distribution of political power owes its articulation and eventual success to Jefferson and the Virginia School.

But underneath policy must be a theory of society, an achievable, real, stable society, one capable of protecting its liberties, in Jefferson's vision, a free society. Jefferson's America was to overwhelmingly agricultural, and with vast open lands to the West, would seemingly remain vastly agricultural. Naturally, Jefferson cast his vision of a free society in terms of the best that agrarian life had to offer. Here the many would reside. Here they would hold the power to stay free. They would be freeholders, independent and many.

In Jefferson's Acardia, each freeholding family would possess a sufficiency of land, a basic tool kit, and a broad set of practical skills. Through the operation of labor, this domestic industry would produce nearly all the goods needed for a decent standard of living, food, clothing, shelter, accouterments and amenities. Through the same self effort, what we would call capital improvements, barns, corrals, sheds, and irrigation, could be produced, generally improving life, what we would call progress. From these conditions of life, come most of the mythical virtues of American national character, self reliance, independence, individuality, industry, practicality, inquisitiveness, frugality, and hardiness. Pretty much the tribal package of virtues.

Everything produced would be for use or use value. Perfect self sufficiency is extremely rare at the primary unit of production. The difference is made up by exchanges of equal use value. Free Trade in its original conception is inherently fair trade. So around freeholding units, communities would appear as towns and villages, centers of exchange and marketplaces. Whatever the freeholder produced was their own, save what remittance was necessary to support whatever minimum government needed in the way of sheriffs, judges, mayors. With political power evenly distributed, and economic wealth normally distributed, the freeholder could stand and deliver, beholden to no one. If a few turned rotten, and made a grab for unequal, artificial power, the sensible many could run them up a tree at the polls and put a stop to their machinations. Jefferson did not foresee how vulnerable such freeholding groups were to financial conquest.

Jefferson's theory of a free society is sometimes called Utopian. This is not accurate. From what archeologists and anthropologists discover, these natural economic and political distributions are the primary conditions of paleolithic and neolithic societies. They are the basic fact of tribal human existence, and obviously worked well for most of human history or we would have never survived to blunder into civilized distortions of these first conditions of human experience. The free society is not Utopian, it is Archetypal. Liberty is not a dream, but a drive bred into human nature.

Jefferson's belief that the naturally free society was the healthiest and most progressive parallels Adam Smith. Both envision liberal conditions of political and economic freedom, a culture of freedom if you will. The principal difference is that Jefferson as a plantation owner made the yeoman his hero. Adam Smith as an urban dweller made the small business man his hero. Both were optimistic, believing that the genius of human nature, if given liberty, will fairly drive and improve human circumstance. Both believed that a culture of freedom produced a social mobility that allowed merit find its place in the social arrangements. No liberal in political and economic philosophy denies the value of hierarchical arrangements in division of labor and social organization. One just keeps it limited and temporary, with plenty of opportunity for merit to rise to its moment without burdening society with the denouement of its offspring. Because of the natural inequality of ability, some freeholders will be poor and others well to do. But other things being equal, namely that economic, political or military power, stay unconcentrated, the proportional differences between poor and well to do will remain stable, with membership changing gradually over the generations. After all, the sons of the well to do often prove fools, and the sons of the poor may be born with uncommon genius.

If this happy, tribal like, free society, cast in archaic modern terms by Jefferson and Smith, is to be preserved and to flourish, it must be protected from the principal threats to those economic and political conditions which make it free. Unequal, self favoring political power might be imposed from above or without, by military arts or the police power of a higher level of government. Or economic monopoly power might be persistently exercised in exchanges of trade, for the profit or gain of the favored franchise, siphoning off the wealth of the community elsewhere. One gets the other. If you have a military occupation of a community, you can take all its wealth as the spoils of war. If you hold the mortgage on the entire county, you can make yourself king.

Jefferson's political philosophy and policy to prevent such events disturbing the natural forces of a free society were straightforward. Extend and protect suffrage, make government small and limited, from state to local, as well as from the federal to state level. Universal voting privileges would insure the even distribution of political power. The voice of the minority would be heard. Minimal government would insure that the government itself could not became the source of unequal power. Afterall, a healthy free society should be able to solve most of its social problems without recourse to the government to enforce their prejudices. Running to the government for petty favors would seem a sign of failure in the culture itself.

In the economic realm, free trade, if fair, would preclude exchanges of unequal power where one party gains at the definite loss of the other, thereby skewing the distribution of wealth into a maldistribution. For example, any surplus use value that crop and livestock farmers of late 19th century America produced was commandeered by the pricing policies of the monopoly railroad transport corporations. Had these exchanges been fair and free, there would be a great deal more capital stock in the American countryside to support rural economy, and a lot fewer skyscrapers in the congested, urban bee hives.

The accomplishments of the Jefferson Democracy are numerous, but the foremost is the Bill of Rights, the ten commandments of human liberty. Regrettably, two historical misfortunes blunted this achievement. First, its present form as ten amendments to a constitution make it look like an afterthought when it should up front setting the conditions and limits of constitutional law. Second, the finest expression of their substance is Thomas Paine's *The Rights of Man*, but his involvement in the French Revolution, and the extremes to which that Revolution went, discredited both Paine and his work. The possibility that the violence there unleashed was evidence of centuries of injustice and abuse at the hands of a privileged aristocracy, viciously enforcing an unnatural, hierarchical society to their permanent advantage, was missed by conservatives and reactionaries of that time. In their eyes, the French Revolution proved that the unworthiness and dangerousness of rule by the masses, thereby justifying their belief that a rigid pyramid structure must be imposed upon society to keep it from disintegrating. Even the liberal democrats were horrified at the fury and chaos. Consequently, the Bill of Rights has been untouched and unperfected. The marginal place of the Bill of Rights in the modern mind is well illustrated by the current flap over the presence and removal of a stone monument of the Ten Commandments in an Alabama courthouse. Would it not be better if judges, jurists, and legislators were confronted by a monument to the Ten Amendments every time they entered their place of business? How many church doors are embossed with the Ten Commandments?

Otherwise, the Jefferson Democracy formed the first national opposition party, eliminated the national debt, killed the First Bank of the United States, extended suffrage, championed international free trade, and expanded the land base of the nation making every citizen's dream of becoming a freeholder a real possibility. These accomplishments and objectives range across both the political and economic spectrums and together were meant to promote and preserve human liberty as far as possible. You cannot say you have liberty and be sure that you have. Only political power, applied through concerted policy actions, can make, or change, the political and economic conditions which create or deny liberty. You have to make society free. Declarations are only words easily construed, twisted, or ignored.

Critiques

At bottom, the position of Hamilton and his exclusionary kind rests on the belief that democracy is inherently unworkable, and that delusional attempts to install it leads nations to ruin and misery. Therefore, societies must be hierarchically structured, with gradations in the curtailment or enhancement of liberty worked out from top to bottom like a pyramid, in order to survive at all, let alone be ordered, stable, and productive.

There is plenty of history to back up this claim if one ignores the paleolithic and neolithic ages of the species. First, nearly all ancient civilizations were blatantly hierarchical. But as all were formed from conquest, this structure may easily be only the consequence of the spoils of war, and not of necessity. The thousand years of feudal Europe was based upon the Germanic conquests that followed the Fall of the Western Roman Empire.

Second, the famous ancient experiments in democracy, the Greek city states, have a mixed record. The fighting power of a freedom motivated soldiery, as evidenced at Marathon, Salamis, and Plataea, and the intellectual and artistic explosions that laid the foundations of Western Civilization, speak well to the prospects of liberally expanding human liberty in society. But many Greek city states were half slave, some 80% slave. Slaves mined the silver of Laurium for Athens, and put food on the table for the Spartans. Also, women were severely segregated, largely confined to separate quarters, the gynaeceum. Further, if the city states were not engaged in petty, self serving warfare amongst themselves, its citizens warred upon each other. Countless vicious and destructive revolutions and counter revolutions were staged between the old or new oligarchies and the rest of the citizen masses. But the Greek city states emerged after waves of conquest and so contained the curse of conquest in the structure of their societies, a privileged class of the few, the descendants of the conquerors, and a subordinate, exploited class of the many, the descendants of the subjugated. Most democratic reforms, which both extended political power to the people and redistributed severely concentrated wealth, were initiated by aristocratic reformers to keep the many from massacring the few. When the Greek masses arose, they were armed, much like the American militia. Curious, though, how often the greatest champions of the people, liberty, and democracy, arise from the privileged few.

Perhaps had the Greeks another two centuries in developing the culture of freedom, in experiencing the leveling effects of democracy and progress, they would have resolved these inherited conflicts. But in the end, unable to act in concert nationally, the Greek city states fell piecemeal before the military onslaughts of Macedonia and Rome, much like Gaul fell before Caesar two hundred years later. This is the fatal flaw of free tending societies, absorbed in their own problems, interests, and opportunities. They are especially vulnerable to the exaggerated power that tyrannical societies are sometimes able to gather and project in wars of conquest. But to turn one's own society into a pyramid of tyranny to match tyranny loses the war and the battle, and misses the point. The serfs of Europe changed their masters many times, but their lot never changed unless they themselves stood up in protest. As they say, live free or die, and many have.

But history also presents compelling evidence that human liberty and the democratic spirit cannot be suppressed, indeed, can pervade whole cultures and civilizations without stunting their progress and evolution. The most interesting are the occasional inscribed boasts of Ancient Near Eastern Monarchs. For example, consider the words of Hammurabi at the end of his famous, carved in stone, legal code.

"I am the guardian governor…In my bosom I carried the people of the land of Sumer and Akkad…in my wisdom I restrained them, that the strong might not oppress the weak, and that they should give justice to the orphan and the widow…Let any oppressed man, who has a cause, come before my image as king of righteousness…may my monument enlighten him as to his cause, and may he understand his case. Let them say of me that Hammurabi indeed is a ruler who is like a real father to his people."

These words breathe with an overpowering empathy with the many, the people, the weak, the poor and the less fortuned. When an absolute monarch, sometimes even thought to be a god himself, with no need to concern himself with human liberty at all, can take such pride in his advancement of the interest of the people, the many, and call it justice, there must be something deeply emotional and powerful in the spirit of democracy, in the fulfillment of human liberty, something deep in the nature of the species. Something as easy to eradicate as teaching a dog not to bark.

History is replete with examples of rebellion and doomed revolutions. The suppressed, oppressed, and subjugated, never seem to get the hang of their condition. Humans seem incapable of adapting finally to tyranny. Spartacus, Vercingeteriox, Toussaint L'Ouverture, the Peasant's Revolt in Reformation Germany, and the overthrow of Apartheid in South Africa, all suggest that the sense and truth of human liberty is an incurable feature of human makeup. You can break the human spirit of some, but not all.

But one could argue that this quirk of human nature is simply unfortunate, and interferes with the formation of the large scale political and economic organizations that bring power, prosperity, progress, and greatness to the nation state. Where is the nation, the civilization, devoted to human liberty and the culture of freedom, that ever reached any high points in art, economy, and intellectual prowess, and still united millions upon millions of people bred to a common language and culture. Greece failed. Are there any other candidates? There is. History knows them as the Celts.

At one time, the Celtic Nation was spread from Galatia into central Anatolia, through Thrace, up the Danube, through the middle of Germany, into Gaul, the British Isles, and the Iberian peninsula. Their cultural high points precede the Golden Ages of the Greeks, and in 387 B.C., they sacked Rome. Had they united through enforced hierarchical power, they could have crushed the Mediterranean World. But they were too imbued in the practice of human liberty to manage such conquest.

In addition to the vast geographical expanse inhabited, Celtic Civilization enjoyed longevity, beginning with the Hallstatt period around 700 B.C. through the La Tene cultural high point after 450 B.C., to the conquest of Gaul by Caesar in the 50's B.C. But the Insular Celts in Scotland, Ireland, Wales, and Cornwall remained free, and to this day, their descendants are well known for their fierce sense of independence and freedom. This devotion to liberty shows itself dramatically in the Pelagian heresy of Celtic Christianity. Like most native peoples who adopted Christianity, the Celts blended it with their own beliefs and rituals. Irish monasticism, with its withdrawal from society and retreat into nature to find and worship God, was one expression of these deeper Celtic beliefs and practices. The doctrines of free will and of a blessed human nature articulated by the monk, Pelagius, was another. But these tenets of faith flew in the dour face of St. Augustine's cold blooded original sin and irrevocable predestination. So the John Calvin of the Early Christian Church relentlessly persecuted the heresy, finally invoking the political power of the Emperor to suppress the Celtic Church. This was why St. Patrick was sent to Ireland. Rome once again trampled on the Celtic celebration of liberty. After all, what is liberty without free will. Eliminate free will, and liberty is moot.

How, then, did these obstinate devotees of human liberty fare? What did they accomplish? Their twice told trouncing at the hands of the vast hierarchically arranged Roman Empire make them look like losers.

To begin with, as a nation, across tribes, provision was made for all people to have access to curative medical treatment, sick maintenance, and hospitals. They had what we would call a national health insurance policy and program. The Celts also developed a highly sophisticated, decorative aesthetic, quite different from existing Near Eastern and Mediterranean aesthetics, though obviously sharing with as well as influencing these other general locations of large scale civilization. They made provision for education as they did with health, though the spread of literacy is difficult to assess. The Celtic intelligentsia, the druids, strictly followed an oral tradition and the development of memory. There is no Celtic literature from its Continental Golden Age, but the vast early Irish literature shows that there was a large, complex body of knowledge successfully transmitted over the long run of generations. The druids were the social glue that crossed tribal boundaries and created a national character. They were the teachers, the poets, the doctors, the judges, the priests, and moral counselors of Celtic Civilization. They had special rank and privilege. But none are known to have built castles for themselves. A druid of proven skill and wisdom could stand between the warrior mobs of two disputing tribes and tell them that they cannot fight on this day, and they all obey.

The Celtic nation was a confederation of dozens of tribal clans. Some were as small as several thousand. The Helvetii that Caesar drove back into the Alps were said to be numbered 350,000. They spoke one language, though with many dialects and accents. They had one common custom of manufacture and technology, though again with local variations. Being closer to the band and tribal scale of social organization, the Celtic law and governance bore strong resemblances to tribal practices. All officials were elected by their peers. The chiefs among the warriors, and the firsts among the druids. They practiced community property law. No absolute private property. No inheritance by primogeniture. They were a mobile people, physically and socially. Merit mattered. They were bred on individuality, on becoming a unique person instead of a clone of common conformity. Power was balanced between the warriors, the druids, and the people, the muscle, eyes, and bone of their society.

For all this decentralization, this diffusion of liberty throughout the nation, the Celts were masters of economic production. The archeological sites are all well provisioned. They obviously flourished in agriculture and animal husbandry for they overpopulated and swept down from the north in mass migrations invading the Mediterranean World. At Manching in Central Europe, a huge industrially organized complex has been unearthed. In the heart of the sixteen square mile layout are dozens of building flats containing rooms, 6 yards wide and 40 yards long, full of the debris of manufacturing operations. This was what we would call today a large scale capital operation, most likely using assembly line schemes and consequently, some standardization of parts. These are all the signs of a society flourishing under the release of actually achieving human liberty on a significant scale, in a nation of millions, a progressing society. If this was accomplished without the aid of banks, so much more the wonder. We have no idea what kind of structure the Celts gave to credit and money, if much at all.

Yet the Celts were twice defeated by Rome and its might of hierarchical power imposed over individual liberty. The Celtic warriors never learned to discipline their tactics and carry through strategy, while the Romans adapted, first fearing the Celts as Hell's Fury unleashed to stabbing them down like cattle to be slaughtered. Still, the Celtic Civilization stands out as dramatic and convincing proof that democracy can govern a great nation and to so well. There is a better alternative to Hamilton's dream of a hereditary ruling class, based on the circumscription of liberty to favor their political power, and living well by siphoning off an extra measure of the economic product of the many, the masses, the common people, the ones that do not matter. Like slaves or serfs, or third world factory workers.

* * * * *

Goethe observed that a man's virtues are his own, while his vices are those of his age. Thomas Jefferson is a perfect specimen of this adage. The American revolutionary political turbulence was blessed with the presence of two broad spectrum, creative geniuses, Benjamin Franklin and Thomas Jefferson. Franklin mastered the miracle of the 1787 Constitutional Convention. To Jefferson fell the lot of creating a true revolution, politically and socially, out of the opportunity created by national independence and new constitutional law. Hamilton and the Federalists had no interest in political reformation. The existing British system was their ideal.

Jefferson's success in leading and establishing a true revolution warrants the title, the Jefferson Democracy. The second American Revolution was the Jackson Democracy. They have been no others, just ad hoc, piece meal episodes of democratic policy and action, Teddy Roosevelt's trust busting, the progressive income tax, the establishment of the social security infrastructure, and the civil rights movement. What is lacking is the comprehensive and simultaneously pursued set of social, political, and economic objectives that once achieved significantly move society in the direction of liberty for all. It takes a democratic revolution to advance human liberty all at once, where power residing in the Common Will is applied over a unified set of across the board actions that roll back the reactionary social organization, and produce the changes in political and economic conditions that demarcate the presence and progress of human liberty.

But neither Jefferson or Jackson were saints. Both were slaveholders, enjoying the expropriation of the slave economic product over large land holdings. They were old school landed aristocracy, Jackson, first generation, Jefferson, third generation. Both were party to the Indian removals to marginal western lands. Unfortunately, right only advances in the midst of wrong. The wrong America inherited from the Old World was considerable.

The European Colonial Slave Trade represents the very worst of economic and political tyranny. Beyond the inherent moral evil of the condition of slavery itself, the true antithesis of human liberty, the Slave Trade was brutally and viciously perpetrated upon a people whose physiognomy was radically different from those who were purchasing mastership, thus making the self serving, sense of godly superiority easy to accept and impose. All for the purpose of the extravagant capital gain possible by expropriating the economic product of the slave population. Enormous amounts of money wealth were generated by the slave plantation system and its black slave trafficking, all neatly funneled to a few, the emerging British moneyed aristocracy that Hamilton sought so desperately to emulate. But there were no slave markets in London. When a tardy moral conscience finally swept Europe and outlawed slavery, the wealth appropriated was in London, and the slaves in America. This was the new capitalist order of Europe with a vengeance. It is always so profitable and easy to expand capital when the worst long run costs are born by others, even society itself.

The curse of slavery still haunts the American landscape. It set an unfortunate standard of human debasement and exploitation. In 1794, Massachusetts, any able man caught on his own was liable to be impressed into seamanship. The British practice of this on the high seas brought on the War of 1812. Had the British won this war, the Yankees might have figured out that the impressment practice was the solution to their factory worker problem. But Napoleon escaped Elba, and down in New Orleans, Colonel Jackson and the western minutemen whipped the British veterans of Waterloo. The will behind liberty and the power of democracy shifted west.

* * * * *

More perplexing than the flaws of Jefferson and Jackson and their times is the fact that both the great leaders of American Democracy came from the cream of the social elite of their day. While both possessed an affinity and a rapport with the common man, both were among the most uncommon of men. The enemies of Jackson liked to portray himas uncouth and rude, but the European diplomats who spent time with him considered him to be the most urbane and well mannered of Americans they knew. So the question begs itself. If the champions of liberty and the leaders of democracy come from the elite, where will the Democracy find its leaders and champions tomorrow? From an elite surely disposed to perpetuate itself into a ruling class, an aristocracy of the assuredly well to do?

The answer lies in the natural selection of merit and the social mobility that comes with a free society. Inherited fortune and luck broker our individual fates, but in a culture of freedom, merit, ability, competence, even goodness, can move, be heard, be seen, and proven.

Any society, to be successful, healthy, and progressive, needs the advantages that large scale, cooperative enterprises provide. What epitaph do you write for the tribe that is drowned in a flood when only a month's worth of combined effort could have built the dam that would have saved their lives and their culture? But even the most decentralized of productive social organizations is, of necessity, hierarchical. The hierarchy is the leverage that produces the necessary, or big, economic advantage. This requires significant, temporary grants of power. For example, among the American Plains Indians on the march, police power to whip the tardy, or even burn the property of those who wander off too far, is given to one of the tribe's warrior societies. But if the tribe disintegrates on the march and falls prey to its enemies, the tribe ceases to exist.

The democratic strategy for hierarchical, cooperative organizations is to limit, vary, and mitigate the agents and effects of power. So the American nomads rotated the police power of the march among different warrior societies. Those whose property got burned were re-supplied by the tribe. And chiefs who bickered, played favorites, and made bad decisions, camped alone. In a free society, we want a generational churning among all social sectors and strata. We want a hefty infusion of new blood and new ideas swamping conventional wisdom and the temporary elite every so often. Jefferson thought that a revolution in liberty should occur every twenty years or so. This may have been his profoundest observation.

Jefferson and John Adams, once bitter enemies, died dear friends, on July 4th, 1828. Neither lived to see the election of Jackson to the Presidency and the inauguration of the Second American Democratic Revolution.

* * * * *

If in the end, the instinct and quest for liberty lie in the unfathomable, self evident reaches of human nature, so do all its opposites. If generosity of spirit, tolerance, and a keen sense of fairness are the bright side of our natures, so intolerance, selfish domination, and cold blooded injustice, are the dark side. We put forward the Golden Rule of Morality, to do unto others as one would have done to oneself, but most of human history seems dominated by the practice of the Anti-Golden Rule, I deserve what others do not. This despite all the efforts of all the founders of the Great Religions to teach us the brotherhood of humankind.

The Noble Savage is a myth. The Celtic rite of passage into manhood was the nailing of a dripping human head onto one's door. The Native Americans tribes gladly did to each other, what the invading caucasian peoples did to them. One could almost believe that the worst original sin is man's inhumanity to other men. When we are constrained in our liberty, we are acutely aware of the injustice, even rationally so. We rebel. But when by fortune, we find ourselves among the privileged few wonderfully benefiting from the oppression of the many, we are sorely tempted to make sure we stay there. Living like kings is a lot of fun.

Consequently, there is no finishing the revolutions in human liberty. Indeed the odds seem so often stacked against them. Through unequal power, applied over the long run, a few can live like gods, while the many other inhabit borderlands resembling the perdition they hope those who put them there will end up. Once the chains are secured, it is difficult to rise up and act in concert. Those geniuses arising among the common that manage such are found out quickly and removed like the tallest ears of cornstalk are taken off the top.

The fight for liberty and democracy is too important to be left to piece meal progress. It needs comprehensive action across the political, economic, and social spectrums of culture and society. The last unified democratic program of philosophy, policy, and effective change in America was the Jackson Democracy.

PART II

The Jackson Democracy

The Jackson Democracy

In 1800, Jefferson ascended to the Presidency, though by the slimmest of margins. By a quirk in the ballot printing, his Vice Presidential running mate, Aaron Burr, the leader of the northern branch of the opposition party, scored as many electoral votes as did Jefferson. The new constitution was immediately tested. The election was thrown to the House of Representatives, where Hamilton swung the vote to his archrival, Jefferson. A Burr Presidency would have been an administration without a keel, as his rise to leadership in opposition to the Federalists was far more motivated by his rivalry with Alexander Hamilton for power in New York, than by deeply held democratic convictions.

The personal animus between Hamilton and Burr grew into hatred. In 1804, after Hamilton had swayed the governorship election away from Burr, using publically insulting words, Burr challenged Hamilton to a duel and killed him. As Burr was a known marksman, and Hamilton was decidedly not, Hamilton's participation in the duel was akin to suicide, and Burr's formally sanctioned murder the same. Hamilton's actual psychological state in this fiasco remains one of history's mysteries. Jackson also killed a man in a duel for insulting his wife, Rachel. He calmly took the first bullet, then gutshot his enemy.

The Hamilton-Burr duel was one of the turning points in American History. Had either Burr or Hamilton remained on the political scene, one or both would have reached the Presidency and had their day welding the highest power in the nation. As it was, Jefferson was followed by twin terms held by Virginia School disciples, Madison and Monroe. By the 1824 Election, every politician in the country was calling themselves Jeffersonian Republican Democrats, or Democratic Republicans, so much had the divisions in policy blended. Henry Clay rose to power in Kentucky, espousing the American System, the Bank, the Tariff, and Internal Improvements. John Quincy Adams groomed himself as a compassionate conservative, in those days called a Whig. Andrew Jackson practiced law in Tennessee, speculated well enough in land live off the plantation system, and got himself appointed head of the militia.

As is natural to creative genius, Jefferson adapted once he came to power. Both the possession of power and the changing social landscape created new conditions and opportunities. A small, limited government might be a good idea, but a weak one was not. Jefferson saw the chance to grab the Louisiana Purchase in a fire sale, and carried it out way ahead of Congressional approval. He used his manifest power to eliminate the national debt and kill the First Bank of the United States. He pressed his state party affiliates to extend suffrage, as much as possible. He consented to the first tariff bill however modest. He confronted and somewhat contained the abuse and slavery of impressment that the British Navy carried out upon American sailors. And he build up his party to national dimensions sufficient to keep the Presidency in the Virginia School for twenty four years.

But it is ever the weakness of democracy to interpret the many as all, so even the privileged few are conceded their due. The old Federalist party went down in flames in its opposition to the War of 1812, but they re-emerged as the Whigs, and steadily won back the key elements of their economic program. Protective tariffs became an institution, private corporations were chartered with monopoly status to carry out internal improvements, and in 1816, the Second Bank of the United States, also a wholly private corporation, was established by Act of Congress.

Meanwhile, Americans kept streaming West in numbers large enough to make the capitalist elite seek to restrict land access while fostering immigration to replenish their work forces. The Old Northwest and Old Southwest filled up with settlers and became States, challenging the old seaboard States for national political power. The Indian Nations standing in the way of this expansion, after a heroic defense of their way of life, were crushed, devastated, and moved out of the way. Once again, a vast, new frontier generation of Americans trained in tribal conditions, many of whom had come west to escape the repressive and suffocating seaboard.

Supposedly the War of 1812 was provoked by rude, condescending British behavior, but cold blooded calculations of national aggrandizement were involved at bottom. With Britain occupied with their life and death struggle with Napoleon, Canada seemed ripe for the taking, and as the Indian Nations would align themselves with Britain, another chance to punish and pulverize them presented itself. The American military effort vacillated from feeble to inept. Washington D. C. was raided. The White House burned. Canada failed to fall, not being at all interested in becoming a part of the expanding States. But the

Indians were decisively defeated in the Northwest, and when the British tried to unhinge the Louisiana Purchase from the American Nation, General Jackson and the western militia soundly beat them at the Battle of New Orleans. The Nation had a new military hero whose credentials were as good as Washington's. It also had a new national debt.

Jackson went on to break the armed resistance of the Creeks in northern Alabama, and invaded Florida to drive the Seminoles into the swamplands, flaunting Spanish authority and setting the stage for the acquisition of that land by the new nation. He put in time as a United States Senator from Tennessee, and by 1824, was considered a landslide candidate for the Presidency.

But Jackson was a Westerner. Way too different and uncontrollable compared to the complaisant colonial bred democrat, and known for his indomitable will and temper. The seaboard establishment feared him, and along with their western agent, Henry Clay, fought desperately to prevent his usurpation of their power. John Quincy Adams fluked into the Presidency. But in 1828, Jackson swept away his opposition, won his landslide, and opened the Second American Democratic Revolution.

The Economic Landscape

The principal fact concerning the early 19th century American economic land-scape was its decisive bifurcation, north and south, into two distinctively different economic systems. In the Seaboard South, from Maryland down, a feudal plantation system evolved and entrenched itself. Like landed aristocracy, a power brokering few acquired vast tracts of land, manned these plantations with slaves, specialized in a cash crop, and lived very well off the wealth the plantation slaves produced. The Seaboard North evolved and entrenched feudal capitalism, feeding off the English Industrial Revolution, itself feeding on American cotton, thus setting the stage for its own industrial revolution. Thanks to the Jefferson Democracy, both these aristocracies in waiting had their troublesome political many, who, where they unanimously voted their common interests, could dramatically change the status quo. For the South, old and new, it was the poor freeholding whites who inhabited the marginal lands. But these had no money, were easily reduced to tenancy, and could have their frustrations redirected into racism.

For the North, the marginal freeholders, too, were a problem, but a new class of the many, the factory worker, was proving more dangerously disruptive. The captive factory worker class was the engine behind continuous production and massive capital accumulation. But when they got together and associated in large numbers, airing each other's grievances at the sporadic subsistence living they were afforded, conditions which a self respecting slave might reject as a repugnant way to live, they were prone to take mob action, stopping production, even engaging in violence. But these serfs of the new capitalist regime were property-less and had no vote. They could be suppressed by force in the name of law and order without much fear of political retaliation. Consequently, the Workingman's Party formed and spread in self defense.

The West beyond the Alleghenies was still largely frontier conditions. Huge areas were still occupied by the unwanted Native American tribes. The Westerners were different from seaboard types, whether from the old northwest or the old southwest, and a source of independent political power that could endanger both the deep rooted systems of the seaboard. But with the Missouri Compromise of 1820, the Mason Dixon Line was drawn across the near West. Above would turn into the feudal capitalist society of the Seaboard North, and below would turn into the feudal plantation society of the Seaboard South, the two halves to meet and contend in the Civil War. The New West, with even more robust frontier conditions, roamed by mounted, native warrior bands, lie across the Mississippi, undivided, a land where the autocrats and dandies never measured up.

Money was the power, North and South. Those holding the concentrations of this new form of wealth made sure that it stayed in the right hands. They did this by securing political power and applying it in service of the Hamiltonian program. The vessel of power was the state chartered, but privately owned bank corporation. In other words, the self avowed ruling class took control of the money supply, and correspondingly, the reigns of power. When the money created was to be shared amongst themselves, it was in the form of credit, stock, and bank drafts, referenced to the hard currency of the time, minted United States dollars. When the money created was to be shared with others, it was in the form of paper money, bank notes in triple digit denominations. The paper currency depreciated faster than the fire wall protected credit money. But if you could get the national government to take the paper in payment, for example, western land, you could absorb the depreciation in the national debt. What was needed was a super, central bank to coordinate all the monetary affairs so that it all worked out all right for the moneyed aristocracy. So Congress chartered the Second Bank of the United States, and placed it wholly in private hands. Nelson Biddle was its dashingly young high priest, the steward of the new concentrations of the money wealth.

With the frenzied energy of a gold rush miner, the money machine pumped out the capital to produce a large scale economic expansion, and a comparable swelling of existing fortunes. In 1819, the house of cards fell apart in panic and depression. This was America's first experience with the financially amplified business cycle. Cycles have always been a part of economic production, partly because humans themselves can push their energies only so far, and partly because of natural cycles in the environment. After three Great Pyramids, the ancient Egyptians built only souvenir copies of the real things. And agricultural production necessarily varies with rainfall patterns, droughts, crop and livestock plagues, soil depletion, and erosion. The financial business cycle is caused by over expanding the money supply well beyond what real production and commercial growth can incorporate as increase. Failures occur in too large a numbers for the system to sustain equilibrium. The money supply contracts like an accordion even more rapidly than it expanded. Like a perverse game of musical chairs, a few hold on to their net worth, while a lot end up with worthless paper. Or if you were a factory worker, you found yourself locked out of your only way of making a living, left with mouths to feed on zero income. In an agrarian setup, you could at least roast and eat the grasshoppers that broke you back down to primitive living.

But in a few years, after the the pain, misery, and suffering had been absorbed, mostly by the many, some of whom were surprised to find themselves not counted among the privileged few, the capitalist game of monetary acquisition revived back up. By 1828, the Hamiltonian program for producing a hierarchical society was well back on track. Creditors could still imprison their debtors for default. It would take a 1832 federal law to remove this curse from the landscape.

Wealth wrapped itself in the vestments of righteousness. Hear the words of a 1836 religious tract, "no man can be obedient to God's Will as revealed in the Bible, without, as a general result, becoming wealthy." To such a mind, the sinfulness of the poor man is self evident. Not even the divine right of kings was so contemptuously pernicious.

The Jackson Uptake

As a statesman, the mind of Andrew Jackson is perhaps the most inscrutable in Western history. Most political leaders with scarcely half his longevity produced copious records of their thoughts, doubts, deeds, and reasons for policy. Jackson seemed never to have wasted a word, in speech or letter. His Bank Veto Message and Farewell Address, both very brief documents, are among the greatest in American Democracy, yet each was laboriously crafted through collective process, Jackson deciding the final wording.

Jackson's gifts were these. He was a prodigious thinker. He could spent hours alone with his long stemmed pipe pouring over a situation. He knew his mind and what he stood for. He understood the power of his will and fame, and used these without stint to achieve his purposes. He was a master of timing. His insight penetrated into the strategic foundations of a situation, and his realism made his own position clear. When he saw an opportunity for action in service of his ends, he set it in his sights and moved toward it without faltering. He did not go running about stirring up incendiary fears. He simply waited until the time was right and acted in accord with his convictions. When he moved, it was invariably right at the deepest and most fundamental structural vulnerability of his opposition. Andrew Jackson can only be known and understood by his actions, which like his words, were never wasted.

And by the words of those who moved in the current of democracy he created. Their nemesis, unnatural, artificial concentrations of wealth. The Jefferson Democracy had pushed political equity to secure economic equity. The Jackson Democracy realized that without economic equity, political equity was a chimera, an adolescent fantasy before the conditioning of industrial serfdom settled the harness on. To Jackson, the distribution of wealth was the overwhelming issue of the day. He saw that if wealth were allowed to concentrate, horde, and inherit, political power would soon fall under its sway, and a democracy of a nation of people, a just, free society, would be impossible. He never got far with proposing the inheritance tax, but that was one of his best ideas. The nouveau rich, like the poor, will always be with us. But in a mobile culture of freedom, born position should scarce survive the next generation. The line of the prince will yield the pauper, and from the line of the pauper, the great man.

In Jefferson's vision, the bulk of society would consist of small freeholders, a condition which would render them economically and politically independent, as well as form sound moral character. With this secure foundation, each would find any invasion of the rights and liberties of others unnecessary. Two flaws in this ideal were becoming apparent. First, not nearly enough of the many were reaching freeholder status, and many of these were scattered throughout the frontier, too isolated to be involved in more than local governance. Those striving for freeholder status were faced with mortgages, contractual payment dates, and compounded interest. Even those free might succumb to the snarls of credit and debt.

Second, if the freeholders' seemingly secure position restrained them from coveting their neighbor's property, no such restraint operated to prevent their properties, their rights, and liberties, from becoming the target of others. Wealth, with its unequal power to command, could assail the freeholder a dozen different ways, through fees, debts, petty taxes, interest, and monopoly. John Taylor, the Virginia School's keeper of the faith, called all this bleeding, taxation.

"Taxation, direct or indirect, produced by a paper system in any form, will rob a nation of property, without giving it liberty; and by creating and enriching a separate interest, will rob it of its liberty, without giving it property."

The problem was not wealth, but the apparently incurable disposition of wealth to geometrically increase its concentrations through the application of unequal power at the unfair cost of others. As John Taylor put it:

"Wealth, like suffrage, must be considerably distributed, to sustain a democratic republic; and hence, whatever draws a considerable proportion of either into a few hands, will destroy it. As power follows wealth, the majority must have wealth or lose power."

Or as others of those writing under the Jackson aegis expressed themselves upon the subject.

William Gouge:

"We have heretofore been too disregardful of the fact that social order is quite as dependent on the laws which regulate the distribution of wealth, as on political organization."

Amos Kendall:

"In all civilized as well as barbarous countries, a few rich and intelligent men have built up Nobility Systems, by which, under some name, and by some contrivance, the few are enabled to live upon the labor of the many."

"Those who produce all the wealth are themselves left poor. They see principalities extending and palaces built around them, without being aware that the entire expense is a tax upon themselves."

Roger Taney:

"It is a fixed principle of our political institutions to guard against the unnecessary accumulation of power over persons and property in any hands. And no hands are less worthy to be trusted with it then those of a moneyed corporation."

James Fenimore Cooper:

"Commerce is entitled to a complete and efficient protection in all its legal rights, but the moment it presumes to control it should be frowned upon and rebuked."

Samuel Allen:

"Trade gave rise to a currency, and credit, and the interest of money, and these, though they produced none of the objects of wealth, of themselves, became mighty instruments of accumulation."

"What could be more dangerous to liberty than transferring the greater part of the landed property of the commonwealth to moneyed capitalists, and turning the independent yeomanry into a helpless and degraded tenancy."

"The laws which govern the economic interests of men...contribute more than government, more than morals, more than religion, to make society what it is in every country."

"What have governments been, and what are they now, but combinations of the rich and powerful to increase their riches and extend their power."

"If you would renovate society, you must begin with its economical relations. The rod of oppressor must be broken, he will not throw it away."

Thomas Hart Benton:

"There are but two parties. There never has been but two parties...founded on the radical question, whether People or Property, shall govern. Democracy implies a government by the people...Aristocracy implies a government of the rich."

To the Jackson Democracy, the causes of the skewed distribution of wealth, and its increasing maldistribution, were buried deep in the structure of the money system itself, in the banking system machinery that defined artificial power and self serving privilege. The nation's money was a public good, not a privately arranged commodity. And they saw an additional evil to go with the creeping maldistribution, the magnified business cycle.

Up and down patterns in economic production have long been a feature of socio-economic systems, old and new. But when the Jacksonians studied the details of the Panic of 1819, they clearly saw the role of the new factor of production, money. They correctly noted its effect in amplifying the natural cycle into a spasm, a severe disruption in the rhythm of production and the general welfare. First, there was a sudden, large scale increase in the money supply, through paper money and credit, which led to a speculation and an overproduction for a demand that did not immediately exist. This led to unsold inventory and debt payment defaults, which then led to factory closings and corporate bankruptcies, throwing the factory workers, now numerous, out onto the street, cut off from even bare bone subsistence living, with only the rats they could catch to feed their children. Meanwhile, the owners of credit could sit back and live off their capital, foreclose, pick up the overbuilt productive assets for a song at liquidation sales, and wait for the turnaround that would flush out the stale inventory with cash. In time, maybe years, they could start up production again with factory workers willing to work for wages even less than they had ever dreamed of working for before. If they were still alive and not gone west. The idea that their workers might be one of their main consumer segments never caught on with the feudal capitalists.

The head and heart of this monetary octopus was the Second Bank of the United States, the nation's privately owned, for profit, central bank. Its twenty year charter was up in 1836. By 1828, all the needed politicians, publishers, and lobbyists had been lined up and well paid to pass its renewal charter. Jackson marked it down for termination.

The Death of the Second Bank of the United States

Making more money from money is pure capitalism. Instead of taking a pile of money and converting it into salable commodities, through either purchase or production, that are, then, converted back into the same amount of money plus some more, the profit, money itself is the commodity, and the interest collected is its profit. This is the world of finance, and its institutions are the banking system and the securities markets.

But many banks operating independently can create financial chaos. What is needed is a bank of banks, the central bank, which has the power to coordinate, stabilize, and discipline the subsidiary front line banks. The problem of preventing the new capitalist financial systems from going into meltdown, or blowing up, had befuddled the Europeans for centuries. But by the early 19th century, finally, the Bank of England was evolving into the premier central bank of the imperialist world. Ironically, this was the same time that the Hamiltonian aristocracy attempted to establish an even tighter financial organization through the First and Second Banks of the United States, only to have the Jefferson and Jackson Democracies kill off their efforts.

A national central bank, in private hands, was the centerpiece of Hamilton's program for establishing and institutionalizing a money aristocracy. In his own words, "…such a bank is not a mere matter of private property, but a political machine of the greatest importance to the State." It would be the tie that bound the government to the business community. Such a bank would have a monopoly over the currency and the money supply, its expansions, contractions, and valuations. It would have control and brokering power over credit, which would decide which capitalists lived or died in times of panic and depression. And as a direct result of this power and control, such a bank could control the general price level, which invariably left the price and wages of labor lagging behind. If all this power, in private hands, were structurally aligned just so, the possession of money capital could be secured, preserved, and agreeably increased at a rate greater than enjoyed by the many, thereby assuring concentrations of wealth that grew geometrically while the shared per capita portion of the many shrank.

Today such power is considered so awesome, indeed such a sacred trust, that central banks are organized in such a way that neither private business or government can directly influence its actions. But in Jackson's time, the central bank was wholly under private authority and was expected to act as an agent of the business community. So were the State Banks, each specially chartered monopolies of their respective legislatures. With the power of wealth creation in its hands, the banking system so constituted saw to it that the legislators responsible for the largess participated in the happy cash flows as refreshing retainers, stock options, and seats on the privileged boards of directors. Relationships that now would be called corrupt, or grievous conflicts of interest, were then thought perfectly acceptable social conduct. How old is the pious Pharisee hypocrite?

Coming into existence in Philadelphia in 1816, the Second Bank of the United States immediately went about its business of functioning as a money machine, overplayed its hand, and precipitated the Panic of 1819. Its first attempt to launch a significant monetary explosion crash landed. Real wealth, as measured in standard of living, actual goods and services, comes from actual economic production. It increases, at best, arithmetically, and is significantly constrained by the scarcity of natural resources, and by the fixed, short run capacity of its productive assets. Money wealth, as measured in cash and credit, can increase geometrically in the mathematical money machine, and has no theoretical limit. Invariably these two independently motivated phenomena fall out of phase. The relative general price level, purchasing power, measures the interactive connection between the two.

In the obsstinate myopia of feudal capitalism, workers were not thought to be the prime consumers. The flush of inflation raises prices, while wages are kept low and fall well behind. How else do you win the capitalist game except by minimizing costs, especially labor? But in the land rush behavior of the industrial capitalists, overproduction occurs, inventory goes unsold, cash flows dry up, and fixed debt payments go into begging default. Even if the business capitalist can repay the money capitalist in cheaper dollars, those dollars are increasingly difficult to come by. Future cash flows that the money machine has counted upon disappear. Production halts while the credit system divies up the unsecured spoils. And the factory worker is throw out into the wilderness of dark streets and teeming, hungry ghettos. In the modern, industrial economy, the workers obtain their living through access to a job, which provides the money with which to procure a standard of living, just as once, the peasant could manage to stave off starvation through access to the land. Not surprisingly, after six months of no job, no money, and long eyed, hungry children, many a factory worker decided to go west and take a chance at becoming a freeholder on the frontier, where steady effort on their part might secure a steady, decent living for self and family. Those that stayed behind expressed their sentiments in bread riots.

But the new national economy recovered. The Bank moderated its practices. In 1832, a bill renewing its charter sailed through Congress on the winds of well rewarded persuasion. Jackson vetoed the bill. Congress failed to override. The Jackson landslide of 1832 made mere passage of renewal bills impossible. As if to prove Jackson's complaint for all history, Nelson Biddle deliberately contracted the money supply, producing a painful national depression. But this final wrath of injured vanity failed. In 1836, the Bank expired by operation of law. Government deposits were distributed throughout the state banking system to start with, but eventually were held in a separate subtreasury unit, removed from the banking system all together. In one swift campaign, Jackson separated business from the government just as the Bill of Rights separated church from state.

When the Jackson Democracy moved into the state legislatures, the state chartered, monopoly banking system was likewise dismantled. In its place, general articles of incorporation were instituted, allowing anyone one with the necessary capital to open a bank. Thus in the same campaign, Jackson established the framework for the competitive, free enterprise system.

These were not small accomplishments. When Adam Smith, in 1776, advocated a small role for government in the conduct of the economy, he had in mind the price fixing and monopoly granting he saw rampant about him, parliamentary actions enforced by the power of the state for the benefit of a few. He did not see that the free market, the free enterprise system, he would put in its place, would itself require strong government to establish and protect it. Privilege is a hard habit to break. Capitalism works quite fine in feudal or fascist societies. Only through free market competition are the benefits of democratic capitalism, mobility in person and wealth, and innovation and progress, possible. The Jackson Democracy is the first real world application of Adam Smith's free enterprise ideas.

Corporations

The corporation is a natural instrument of capitalism. In fact, it is vital to a successful free enterprise system. Without the corporation, the number of competitors is limited to the number of individuals wealthy enough and willing to play the capitalist game. By pooling numerous smaller capital stakes, a corporation emerges that is strong enough to compete vigorously in the marketplace. By the same mechanism, the wealth generated is more widely distributed that would be the case if all free cash flows went to one lord patriarch. Further, when the corporation dies in bankruptcy, its assets are not passed on through inheritance, but are sold outright on the auction block. So while the corporation is a hierarchical organization, it is capable of involving the many, sharing with the many, and is temporary, properties which are well in line with democratic capitalism. But it has flaws. For example, like capitalism, it is value free. When granted limited liability, the corporation is also an excellent instrument of plunder.

In tribal society, power, authority, and wealth, came under direct public inspection. Private conscience and public morality were intimately connected. Public amorality was not possible without demeaning personal rebuke. Both Jefferson and Smith count on this tribal unity of private and public morality to keep society and its economic and political business honest. For Jefferson, the hero of such a cultural ethic was the freeholder. For Smith, it was the owner, manager, and the first worker, the fabled sole proprietor, who, by living amongst his customers, made sure that the pride of ownership showed up in clean premises, quality work, and fair dealings. Reputation matters a great deal to real persons when they must publicly face the consequences of their actions.

In contrast, though granted the legal status of personhood to insure the operations of contracts, the corporation is not personal. The stakeholders vote in a board of directors, the voting strength proportional to the size of the stake risked. The board of directors then hires the executives who will actually manage the corporation's business. Ownership and management are divorced. Smith was suspicious of this separation for it protected private conscience from guilt that would come from an actual personal acquaintance with the corporation's real business conduct. As a Massachusetts Legislative Committee observed:

"These artificial creatures, unlike employers, are not chastened and restrained in their dealings with the laborers, by human sympathy and direct personal responsibility to conscience and to the bar of public opinion."

The owners of corporations never have to see the hole in the ground that the action of their money has left behind. They need only deposit the distributed dividends. This schism trumps the democratic tribal constraint of public purview and personal public accountability. This is a serious problem for both stakeholders and the public at large. Management, as Galbraith has well explained, becomes a power class in its own right, and has interests of its own that it will serve before considering the interests of others, be they stakeholders or citizens. These interests at best are self centered, and are often amoral, that is, valuing any self interest without equally valuing the consideration of the interests of others. Whether through absentee ownership control, or secretive management overseers, the corporation can operate without aligning its interests with the nation, the state, the people, the public, its customers, or even its own employees, the job tenants of the corporation's cash flow landscape. If the jobs are the beast of burden jobs, the old working class jobs, the tenants can be held in so low esteem that they can be murdered and driven off by the national military, provided, naturally, that the government is working for the corporate interests. The Robber Barons of the American Industrial Revolution did just that. Even within the free enterprise system, they achieved Hamilton's program. Their names are still hallowed today.

But in Jackson's time, the use of government power to franchise a corporation, grant it monopoly, and then make it untouchable, was the present problem. At both the state and federal level, corporations were being specially chartered to manage and profit from government funded internal improvement projects, like roads or bridges. The opening move in ending the policy of government aid to private corporations came in 1830 with the veto of the government subscription of stock in the Mayville turnpike corporation in Kentucky. One would have thought that Jackson had crucified Jesus all over again for all the outcry from those losing their special advantage. But the separation of government and business was underway, culminating in the Bank Veto and the spread of general articles of incorporation allowing anyone who could raise the capital to engage in business, thus establishing the competitive, free enterprise system.

Government aid and involvement in private business is inherently ambiguous. Depending on intents and purposes, it can support feudal capitalism, fascism, socialism, or democratic capitalism. The task before the Jackson Democracy was to break the power of the incipient feudalism capitalism seeking to entrench itself. Separating private business from the power and favor of government marshaled at its bidding was pressing need at the time. It still is.

The next step was to secure the new policy of free enterprise and the public good through judicial review. This was accomplished in 1837 by the Supreme Court ruling led by Chief Justice Roger Taney, a Jackson man. In Massachusetts, under old monopoly law, the Charles River Toll Bridge fed both Beacon Hill and Harvard University. The new democratic movement wished to build a new bridge, the Warren Bridge, with public access. The Charles River Corporation sued for breach of contract. Taney's written opinion against opened the door for the government to act for the general public welfare, while making the competitive, free enterprise system itself a public good. This judicial foundation lasted until the Civil War. In the subsequent, Robber Baron triumph of feudal capitalism over the free enterprise system, the judges grew rich, and voted their master's interests.

This was not known in Jackson's time, that unsupervised capitalism, combined with weak, even supplicant, government, would destroy or swallow its competition, even in a free market set up. The correction of this imbalance would await the inexplicable career of Theodore Roosevelt.

The Freed Factory Serf

It can hardly be expected that an industrial capitalism arising out of an entrenched feudal society would view its new working class any differently than the medieval barons viewed their serfs, or masters, their slaves, that is, as beasts of burden to be used in achieving its ambitions of wealth accumulation. When Adam Smith enunciated the labor theory of value to justify fair wages for labor, he also consigned labor to supply and demand market dynamics. He failed to foresee the extreme conditions a labor market can take on. In his world of village and town capitalism, supply and demand were equal enough for one to think that the equilibrium price of labor would approximate just wages. But when you enclose the commons, and expel the peasants who have been eking out a living there for centuries, when you enlarge tenancy, and by hard rents, make extended families unviable, sending even more poor souls to the towns and cities in search of jobs that might save them from starvation, you create a super glut in the supply of labor. In such a market, the forces of supply and demand are wildly and unnaturally unequal. Labor can be had for barely subsistence wages, easily sunk into company debt, made to work man killing hours, and fired at will. Unlike the slave or the serf, the factory worker severed from their living was no concern or responsibility of the former employer. As the new working class was segregated by living quarters, they were easy to keep out of sight.

Both David Ricardo and Thomas Malthus, prominent English writers in political economy after Smith during the time of Jackson, took this historically driven labor glut for granted. They examined the motivations and alternatives of the desperate workingman, and concluded that subsistence wages were inevitable like some iron law. A hungry, family man will work for just enough to bring enough bread home to keep the family alive one more day, when his alternative is to move into marginal lands, or the modern urban wastelands, where scavenging and gathering is the mode of survival. But in America, there was also the option of moving West to the frontier and taking a chance of making it as a freeholder, beholden to no one. The factory workers who stayed behind organized early and became a political force as the Workingman's Party. Jackson welded these to his Democracy. In time, they became a separate, more radical political party, the Loco Focos. Curious how the more closely a person's, or a group's, positions resemble the New Testament teachings against riches and for brotherhood, the more they are labeled radical and extremist.

The favored and their shills would always like to believe that the distribution of wealth is dictated by the economic system, thereby sacrosanct and inviolable, as if society had no other purpose to uphold than that economic regime, as if government were to be only of the system, for the system, and by the system, as if the present system had been handed down from Mt. Sinai, as if it were the Will of God that the richer become richer and the poor poorer. They would explain the munificence that befalls them as the result of their virtues, but it is precisely their lack of virtue that causes the maldistribution of wealth in the first place. There is a alternative called equitable sharing, the just price of Thomas Aquinas. Its neglect is a matter of choice, not necessity. As John Stuart Mill observed:

"It is not so with the Distribution of Wealth. That is a matter of human institution solely. The things once there, mankind, individually or collectively, can do with them as they like. They can place them at the disposal of whomsoever they please, and on what ever terms...The distribution of wealth, therefore, depends on the laws and customs of society. The rules by which it is determined, are what the opinions and feelings of the ruling portion of the community make them, and are very different in different ages and countries, and might be still more different, if mankind so chose."

As observed in Part I, one can empirically judge the social justice of a society by examining its distributions of political rights and economic wealth. There can only be one just and fair distribution. Will there be a nation of people, or just a sovereign incorporation of a gilded aristocracy?

Must wages be regrettably set by the existing conditions of supply and demand automatically? Hear Matthew Carey's answer in writing for the Workingman's Party.

"But I contend for it that every principle of honor, justice, and generosity, forbids the employer to take advantage of the distress and wretchedness of those he employs, and cut down their wages below the minimum necessary to procure a sufficiency."

In the winds of the Jackson Democracy, the rights of the new working class were recognized. They organized into trade unions and went on hundreds of strikes for better pay, decent working conditions, shorter hours, and for payment in cash instead of company scrip. Even the children walked out once, on their own, to the cheers of their parents, when their lunch hour was moved from noon to one. But most strikes failed. The ringleaders of the children were fired. Real collective bargaining power lay a hundred years ahead in the New Deal. But the legality of unions was established in 1840. Suffrage was extended and protected. The secret ballot was introduced, poll taxes were reduced, and the sunset laws, which closed the polls at sundown when all honest laborers were still locked up in their jobs, were repealed. Under the Van Buren follow up administration, the ten hour day was made federal law. The national government would set the standards of decency on behalf of the people, leading by example. On intellectual and cultural grounds, the most interesting accomplishment of the Jackson Democracy was its nurturing of the international utopian capitalism that briefly flashed upon the British and American scenes in the early 19th century.

Before Adam Smith invented economics, he was renown for his work in moral philosophy, and was a guiding spirit in the Scottish Enlightenment. That movement was founded on the belief that science, industrialism, and the humanities could be harmoniously united in a free, decent, and progressive society. Robert Owen took the theory and turned it into practice.

Owen was a successful capitalist manufacturer who apparently believed the New Testament ethic to be reasonable and possible. He believed that you could treat your workers well, even generously, and they would still be productive and profitable, maybe even more so. At New Lanark, Scotland, he established a community around a factory system that paid well, provided decent, affordable housing, schools, and other healthful social services. Visitors came from all over Europe to see the strange new zoo animal, these denizens of the lower classes who were well fed, washed, literate, and happy, and still motivated to work at a job without grumbling or resentment. Owen sold out handsomely and brought his ideals to America during the Jackson Democracy. At New Harmony, Indiana, he tried to build another ideal community, this one communal, but after a few years, it fell apart. As the rich never learn, neither do reformers. Reform must grow up from the grassroots. When transplanted and imposed from words from a bible beyond a foreign sea, it presumes too much of human nature, both inside and outside the experiment. Making any plan stick on the frontier is like trying to build sandcastles in a rising tide.

Though Owen proved the positive reality of democratic capitalism at New Lanark, his failure in utopian capitalism at New Harmony, while stirring up the sentiments of American labor reformers, made him easy for the serious minded to dismiss without second thought as to his accomplishments. He had no successors, no converts among the capitalist rich. What a different America, indeed world, it would had the robber barons Teddy Roosevelt busted taken Robert Owen as their role model instead of John Calvin. Would Hilter's fascist capitalism have even been possible then?

Hard Money

As trade grew, civilization advanced. Each fueled the other. But large scale trade through barter exchange processes is bulky, cumbersome, and complicated. The value of a simple, convenient medium of exchange was readily apparent, and so money was invented. With money comes capitalism. Merchant capitalism is as old as money. Quantities of the new medium are used to acquire goods that can be resold at higher prices, thereby increasing the original capital. The capitalist game does drive economic activity, whether it be commercial or industrial, and in the process, goods are produced and made available, enriching society's standard of living.

Perhaps the ancients intuitively understood the prime directive of money supply management, that it be kept proportional to the actual production of goods and services that will be exchanged. Any significant increase or decrease relative to real production has destabilizing consequences, socially, politically, and economically. At any rate, they settled upon the scarce, precious metals as money, which being a commodity, could only be increased through means of real production, and therefore, limited to the arithmetic growth rates of real production.

The mirror of money wealth kept pace with real wealth, and neatly under control of the monarchs who then funneled it into the economic system by spending it. Until the invention of interest, geometric expansions in the money supply, except by conquest, then concentrated in the hands of a few, were not possible.

In Jackson's time, money was in the middle of its transition from hard, concrete, commodity based forms to soft, abstract, mathematically based forms. The transition began with the appetite of the European aristocracies for Oriental luxuries that had to be paid for in gold money. This loss of capital caused prices to fall continuously, bringing the usual distress and discouragement to production and trade. Enough pain to send them out into the monster infested oceans to find sailing routes to India and China, where the luxuries originated. They found India, and then the New World trying for China straight across the Atlantic. The theft of New World gold, where the commodity was used more for ornament than money, taught the Europeans the other side of money supply. One fully laden Spanish convoy brought home more gold ingots than the Old World possessed in all its efforts up until the time of the theft. Prices in Spain soared. England, through successful piracy, next caught the new disease, and soon the whole European continent was awash in vast new quantities of money wealth. The new, emerging industrial capitalism was well provisioned. At the same time, the paper draft, credit system was reviving with the Banks of Italy, Amsterdam, and England. Their new power in increasing the money supply, and its stimulative effects on real production and commerce, spurred the Great Nation States in their imperial and economic conquest of the rest of the world.

Once money becomes mathematical, its tokens intrinsically worthless, its supply can be expanded at a far greater rate than can be achieved by the production of a real, commodity based money supply. A flash flood in money produces a characteristic sequence of events. First of all, the influx falls into the hands of a few who are able to use it took take initial positions on the prospective landscape of economic growth. But as productive growth is mostly only a promise and hope to begin with, much of the excess money ends up being used in placing bets on the collections of productive assets, corporations, that look like they will handsomely succeed, thereby securing lucrative long run cash flows for the shareholders. Share prices bid up on mere forecasts of earnings which realistically may still be years away, even if all the risks are overcome. This is mass speculation, and its bubble of artificial money wealth can get no larger than the new money fueling it. For as the prices of productive assets, real and potential, rise before one's eyes, the practice of short terms loans becomes profitable. Obviously, when the money stops, the price rise must hit a ceiling and level off, probably somewhere around the general price rise the subsequent inflation gradually brings about. But for some intransigent reason, wages and paychecks never keep up with the rise in commodity prices. Distress strikes the society, the greater fool hides in his hole, and the dreams of riches collapse in real space and time. As equity prices sink back to normal, short term loans are called in, fire sale liquidations of financial assets occur, and money disappears as fast as it appeared. A massive redistribution of wealth takes place. And the brunt of consequent economic depression is borne by those laid off from their jobs and thrown into the morass of the ghettos and warrens, and borne again by those lucky enough to work themselves to death for starvation wages. This drastic stop and go action of loose money capitalism repeats with discouraging frequency, usually severe at least once every generation. The whole idea of tying paper money to the gold standard was to re-establish the constraint of commodity based production on the creation of money. But the gold standard failed. Mathematical money is all we have today.

The intellectual wing of the Jackson Democracy understood this new phenomena in money supply perhaps better than any one until Milton Friedman. But their approach to resolving the problem was highly original. They sought to divide money into two classes. Hard money, for taxes, wages, land sales, and general store retail. And soft money, for the business community to circulate amongst itself as proved convenient and useful in their arrangements of proprietorship, as well as confined to themselves. Let the capitalists play with the volatile mathematical money, but restrict the damage of any accident to their class. Let the common, the many, know that the money they earn will be good enough to buy them a livelihood they can count on. This is the essential compromise democratic capitalism must make. First secure the general welfare by securing the laborers in the fruits of their labor, protecting them from the debilitating, unnecessary consequences of mathematical money manipulations run amok. Then harness the vitality of capitalism with the competitive, free enterprise system, and let the capitalist players work out whatever purely financial arrangements amongst themselves as they find useful, providing these are not used to bilk the many through their soft money schemes.

By eliminating the private central bank, and taking firm control of the hard money supply to the point of driving out all bank notes below $20, Jackson sought to re-structure the economic relations of the society in favor of democracy. He expected his actions to moderate the business cycle so obviously aggravated by the fluctuations of mathematical money, and to restrict, or prevent, the artificial transfer of wealth from the laborer and the farmer to the business community. In his own words:

"…thus a metallic currency be ensured for all the common purposes of life, while the use of bank notes would be confined to those engaged in commerce."

After Jackson, the theory and policy of a two tiered money system was lost under the international sway of the gold standard compromise between hard and soft money. But in his brief time, Jackson used the substantial presence of both hard and soft money, and deliberately manipulated their relationships to promote democratic objectives. In this Jackson was a lone pioneer like Robert Owen, but also with Owen, ranks as one of the founders of democratic capitalism.

Freeholding and the Frontier

Jefferson was never fond of Jackson. He had the unblooded intellectual's dubious fear of the masterful man of action. But Jackson was a creation of Jefferson's freeholder vision. He came of age in the West and instinctively understood the democratic promise held in a sufficiency of independent freeholders. He wanted a homestead act from the beginning.

Under the existing land sales laws, the $1.25 per acre seemed affordable, but the $200 sum needed to secure a minimum quarter section was well beyond the poor who needed access to land just to survive. Most sales went to land speculators, and before the hard money legislation were often paid in bank scrip that soon became worthless. Offering the land free to those who would earn their equity through sweat would turn the frontier into a freeholder's proving ground. Those possessing the fortitude, the self reliance, and can do intelligence, who were still standing five years later, would be the new original Americans. The New West would then send a third wave of democracy through the nation, just as the old West had produced the Jackson Democracy.

Neither the factory or the plantation capitalist favored the homesteading idea. One feared the sudden, mass exodus of their factory workers to the promised land, faster then they could import starving Irish immigrants. The other needed large, contiguous tracts of prime land to make the slave plantation work, and to keep their noisome freeholders confined to the marginal lands. Had homesteading been introduced into the Old South, the Civil War would have been unnecessary. Slavery would have died an economic death. As it was, Lincoln finally snuck the Homestead Act through during the Civil War, to offset his general selling out to the business republican interests.

The New West, the West of fable and legend, would never form a coherent political identity sufficient to support a third American Democratic Revolution. The bloodshed of the Kansas-Nebraska border would divide it as wickedly as the Old West had been divided along the lines of slavery, and the Civil War would cut it off from its natural democratic sources, the free, fresh flow of freeholders. When the War ended, the conquerors set about the West and the South to collect their spoils. The curse of slavery would take its revenge. The revenge of John Wilkes Booth would also curse the nation and cost it its best chance at a third Democracy, Lincoln's.

Lincoln was known for his racially based problems with black Americans. He wanted to send them back to Africa, where he thought they belonged. But Lincoln was also perhaps the most real, intimately sensitive President the country has had save Franklin Roosevelt. Had Lincoln lived, he would have had to experience the black man and woman as they were, often, in person. He would have seen in them what they themselves proved a hundred years later when Rose Parks refused to go to the back of the bus. In his musings after victory was finally secured, he promised to take a look at the factory workers plight. The burden of War had been lifted from him, and he saw his course ahead. The common freeholder American was deep in Lincoln. He did indeed split enough rails to feed his great frame. He did learn how to clerk a store, and did find a copy of Blackstone's *Commentaries* in the bottom of a lot barrel. From the study of this work, he learned enough lawyering to marry, and eventually won a big retainer from a railroad corporation. Lincoln knew the American Landscape. If Lincoln had proved able to take back the country from the victorious military-industrial complex of his day, he may have become the leader of the third American Democracy, to follow Jefferson and Jackson. But as foretold in his dreams and premonitions, this greatness was not to be his.

The Jackson Democracy waned long before the Civil War. The unity of the Westerner was ruthlessly divided, north and south, between free and slave. Its lasting mark on American History, like Jefferson's Louisiana Purchase, was in the continental expansion of the United States. Artfully, Jackson sent Sam Houston to Texas, and when independence was lucked into, held back on annexation, until the fruit had ripened. This happened as the Mexican War, provoked by

Polk, under the banner of Manifest Destiny, and gave America its second coast and its first gold rush. The population of Native Americans in California went from half a million to mere thousands, making Jackson's Indian Removals acts of charity.

Critiques

The Indian Removal policy, as a solution to the Indian Problem short of genocide, began under Jefferson, and was ruthlessly finished under Jackson. Democracy was a still a matter for white people only. There were no high points in the new nation's treatment of the native peoples. All are tragic stories, but the fate of the Cherokee is perhaps the saddest of all.

The Cherokee had amazingly reached the collective decision that to survive in the white world, they must adopt white ways. They did this thoroughly. They developed an alphabet for their language, published newspapers, built their government on suffrage, and grounded their economy on enterprise. A Cherokee town of the time would have looked much like any other American town, save its inhabitants were native instead of migrants. This flattery of imitation did not save them. The lands they occupied were too desirable. Their titles were extinguished by the tyranny of foreign law, their people dispossessed. Search all world history and you will not find another such case of an aboriginal people making such a profound adaptation to survive the coming flood of some one else's civilization. The Cherokee were systematically moved West to Indian Territory, allowed to take only what they could carry on their backs, thousands dying along the route, mainly the old, the young, and the weak. Their Fate was the Trail of Tears.

* * * * *

All through the strategies of Hamilton and the counter strategies of Jackson, the business community is painted in homogenous colors. Its interests are invariably aligned with the money aristocracy, the propertied class, the privileged class, or the class where all the concentrations of wealth and power coagulate. This is too simple. First of all, capitalism is a scheme relating money and productive activity where the gain in exchange is registered as money. The so called lower classes practice it as assiduously as the so called capitalist classes. Second, the interests and playing conditions of small business is not always the same as that of big business. Ask any small town druggist trying to compete with a super discount store's pharmacy. Third, the mathematical production of money, and the position and power such creation provides, places manufacturers, who can only grow through real time and space production, at a cash flow disadvantage. The financial community can suck a manufacturing capitalist dry as easily as it can turn a freeholder into debt ridden serf.

The problem is not business, but unequal power. The small businessman is Adam Smith's capitalist freeholder, and stands in the same relationship to the super sized corporation as the agrarian freeholder stood to the large scale landholder flush with cash. Both face unequal power. Small businessmen band together and send a lobbyist to Washington to plead their cause, when the multinational corporate states can send a dozen each. Surplus money, wielded in the hands of those who control its credit backing, can be used in hostile takeovers of real production enterprises by those whose interests have nothing to do with real production. Small businessmen identifying themselves with the partisan party favoring big business because they think they belong is like farmers voting Republican because they think cheap food policies are good for business.

Democracy levels power. Tyranny concentrates it and employs it ruthlessly to secure its exclusive self serving interests.

* * * * *

Capitalism in its pure, pristine form is simply money driven production that operates somewhat like a board game. A pile of money called capital is used to establish a production process for a commodity which is to be exchanged for money. What the money buys in the way of plant and equipment, and other productive assets, is also called capital, and the act of purchase is called investment. Score is kept by counting up the money before and after. If you have more money afterwards, the difference called profit, you are winning the game. If you have less, called a loss, you are losing. If the capitalist game is played within the context of the free enterprise system, greed and obsession are harnessed in service of the Public Good. Production is intensified. Goods and services are made in abundance. Competition drives the capitalist to produce the best quality at the most affordable price in the greatest quantity, for that is how you win the game in a free and fair business environment. As a consequence, capitalism embraces and seeks to develop large scale operations, or what is now called mass production and mass marketing. If half a population is barefoot, capitalism will produce shoes enough for all. In the early stages of an advancing capitalist civilization, the benefits of money driven production is dramatically evident in an overall, rising standard of living every one can see.

But capitalism has no inherent sense of sufficiency. The influx money that makes the winning score must be sustained. The capitalist does not shoe the populace and call it a job well done. The game continues, and more is its creed. If all have one pair of shoes, a need for two, or three, pair is discovered. One insane human from the ruling class variety is on record for possessing 10,000 pairs of shoes. Once fundamental needs are met across society, spurious needs are invented and filled, until even wholly frivolous needs are indulged to excess. To possess a thousand shoes more than one can ever wear, let alone wear out, is to waste the resources and benefits of the economic production bound up in the reality of the commodity. But capitalism has no inherent sense of waste, except in its own production process. Any costs that can the pushed outside their accounting box of revenue and expenses are gladly forgotten.

Thus, once a society is affluently saturated, the only resort a capitalist has to keep the money flowing is to increase the frequency with which consumers buy, or have to buy, the commodity in question. There is no incentive in making things last. The waste is absorbed elsewhere. The saving and reallocation of productive resources to other needs is not a consideration. There is every incentive in making things cheaper, obsolete, or soon broken down beyond repair. In reductio absurdum, the perfected capitalist economy would produce everything needed, all to be replaced in one year, replicating the gross domestic product in total each year. The long run consequences to the general welfare of such compulsive production strategy is dubious at best.

Pure capitalism has no limit because mathematical money has no limit. It has no natural equilibrium point. Like a rocket without a gyroscope, it can go anywhere, land anywhere, without any purposeful sense of destination. The guidance system for capitalism must come from somewhere else. Without the contextual control of a free and fair enterprise system, the long run of pure capitalism is absurd and terminal. In the final hour of the ultimate monopoly game, the winner sits atop all the money in the world with nothing to buy but a very large hole in the ground.

Essentially, capitalism, save for money, is value neutral. Like the sociopath and the chameleon, it adopts the colors of the society which gives it reign. Its contribution toward good or ill is defined by the value system of the society within which it operates. And there, there are only two choices, two directions, toward democratic capitalism or capitalism at the employ of tyranny. The choice is not between capitalism and something not capitalism. It is between which political regime of capitalism will hold sway in society.

PART III

The Long Night of American Democracy

The Long Night of American Democracy

Philosophers and prophets have long observed the problem of consistency between word and deed. Words can speak of noble virtues actual conduct belies.

America has often held itself forth as the world's great experiment as a nation guided and governed by democratic principles. There are many fine words in American intellectual tradition on the subjects of liberty, justice, and democracy. But real American Democracy after Jefferson and Jackson has been far more a matter of a strangely irrepressible, yet apparently uncoordinated, series of spontaneously generated movements or events, that somehow managed to survive, even cause progress, despite serious efforts to disregard, or stamp them out. In 1899, and again in 1929, any fulfillment of American Democracy seemed forever doomed. The real marvel is that so much progress has been made without the concerted, coordinated, and across the board programs of policy and action that distinguish the Jefferson and Jackson Democracies. One could be tempted to believe that a full, free, and just democracy, a wholly new kind of human society, is the the Manifest Destiny of the North American Continent. Unfortunately, the darkest hour may have just begun.

* * * * *

The house divided could not stand. What is the promise of democracy in a society that condones and lives off slavery? Britain outlawed slavery in 1807. Had not the South been so fire breathing, slavery in America might have lasted another two generations. But it is difficult to believe slavery could have survived into the 20th century. Shame enough that it lasted so long as it did.

The Civil War set American Democracy back a hundred years. First, the men of the many turned away from their fight for social justice, and in patriotic romanticism, enlisted en masse in the national cause. Hundreds of thousands of the bravest gave up their lives, as many to disease as to bullets and bayonets. In one of the ironies of history, the new money aristocracy, unlike the old landed aristocracies of Europe, shunned war, bought substitute bounty men to serve in their place, and cynically gorged themselves on wartime profiteering. By the time the War was over, the modest gains of the working class had been lost. The next round of labor movements would not be nearly as peaceful and bloodless as those of Jackson's time.

Second, the division of the Old West into North and South, free and slave, destroyed the regional unity of the Old West that might have acted as a counter balance to the seaboard power. Whatever synthetic influences its frontier driven values might inject into the nation were lost. What democratic spirit frontier conditions might nurture moved to the New West, from the Great Plains to the Pacific.

Third, the total victory of the northern feudal industrial capitalism over the southern feudal plantation capitalism was the victory of one ruling class over its rival. Hamilton's Federalist spawned aristocracy, the Washington to Boston corridor, held sway and could do anything it wanted with the country to its pleasure. This is the time when the fathers of the robber barons began building homes in the District of Columbia to better watch over their political servants.

Fourth, to win the War, Lincoln had to sell out the country to the industrial capitalists. They got everything they wanted. The best he could do was to hire Edward Stanton as Secretary of War to act as a watch dog with enough bark to dissuade the more flagrant deeds of corruption. Whether Lincoln could have won back the country for the people is a question history never tried.

In the free for all run up to 1899, Hamilton's program, minus the national debt, was zealously followed. The financial system was deeply integrated with the production system and its cash flow, and through their concentration and control of capital, the moneyed elite discovered they could unite to destroy or acquire their competition, sector by sector, and achieve monopoly power without government franchise. The free enterprise system was defeated. This is the era of the robber barons, accurately named, and they had the government in their pocket, no matter the party in power. They saw the power and profit that lay in controlling the transportation grid, and took over all the railroads. They invited mass migrations of Europe's poor and helpless to swell the ranks of their factory serfs. Even these, supposedly conditioned to Old European ways, rebelled. In 1877, a national railroad strike, lead to an epidemic of strikes by workers in many other business sectors. The U.S. Army killed a few and ushered the rest back to work.

Such bloodshed continued through Homestead, Ludlow, to the killings at Henry Ford's River Rouge masterpiece of mass production in 1932.

In addition to importing a pliable migrant factory class, the new nobility of America imported Social Darwinism, the creed to justify their position, conduct, and pretense. As usual, the poor, the unfortunate, and the otherwise excluded many, were to blame for their condition. They were failures in the survival of the fittest game. The winners were obviously superior, deserving of their unequal power and position, and assured a place in heaven to boot. Unjust societies all develop self serving religions, whether secular or sectarian.

From the vantage point of 1899, America, if given another hundred of the status quo, seemed certain to look like Old Europe a hundred years before. History would vindicate Hamilton's beliefs. What progress in the way of democracy would result from a odd mixture of disrupting historical events deriving from the common people and the West. The leaders would be more fitted for the times than fitting the times to their visions of a free and just society.

After the Gold Rush

To begin with, a gold rush is essentially anarchy. Sutter's Mill and Ranch were stripped clean of anything useful like a plague of locust finish off a field of grain. In a money based capitalist society, mining a pile of gold or silver is to achieve freeholder status, at least temporarily. In the California Gold Rush of 1849, 400,000 newcomers, mostly strangers, arrived in one year. But just as in the State of Nature of the classical political philosophers, the more productive conditions of order beg. So the miners, the rushers, created on the spot, local governance. Courts were established with spontaneous jurisdiction, claim regulations were codified into law, and marshals were hired to give the law a gun. Frontier conditions, if left free, breed democracy. The gold rushes of the West were accompanied by the homesteader migration, and the cowboy horse culture, all democracy ridden cultures, the breeding grounds of human liberty.

The West was a potentially more powerful and unmanageable rival to the Old North's nouveau, feudal ruling class hegemony than were the southern rivals just recently subjugated. The West had its own money, and possessed a natural wealth that would enormously enrich anyone who got a corner on it. But old and new money marry. Gold must be shipped to the government to be made into minted, legal tender. Corporate networks can lay a spider web of ownership schemes over the national wealth. And the government was well in the hands of the Grand Old Party. Even Democratic President Grover Cleveland promised to shine their boots and sent in the troops to stop the riots, strikes, and uprisings their uncompromising greed provoked. Corporate profit, corporately held private property, would be held sacred over public property, even over private, personal property too small to be of consequence. With the closing of the Land Office Frontier in 1890, the turbulence of a freely forming democratic society could be locked in and halted.

The combination of an integrated system of corporate organization and control over the money supply, the government, and the transportation grid, fueled by an extravagant sense of entitlement, of deserving unequal power to favor privilege at the cost of others, proved overwhelming. By the late 19th century, the entire economic system was organized into monopoly trusts, sector by sector. Prices and wages were fixed accordingly. With control of the Jackson hard money system, the new financial barons held money constant while the population and the volume of trade grew. This added the subtle interest of deflation to the real interest already assured by contract. The many could not own, and if they did, were soon unable to keep. The nation was reduced to tenancy dependent upon the few. The government servants obligingly looked the other way. New gold was shipped East, and the real wealth of the West transformed into commodities that could be sold in Eastern markets, and thus turned in money which could then be easily transferred to the owners of the cash profit flows. The entire nation would be run like an intra-national colonial system. This was Mussolini's corporate fascism twenty years before El Duce. Democratic Capitalism was smothered in the cradle. Hamilton's feudal elite looked permanently entrenched.

As John Taylor had foreseen, concentrated, money based economic power trumped supposedly equal political power. Unless the aspiring freeholder many could keep and protect its own capital, or the job worker granted capital interest in the fruits of their labor by a new social contract, the returns of real wealth to its labor producers would be reduced to subsistence wages while the government backed trusts ripped off the surplus to leverage the grand lifestyles of a regal nobility. This bestial, nose in the sky regime of feudal capitalism drove the working class to epidemic strikes and bitter uprisings, most repressed by the national army, who were more reliable than the militia who tended to sympathize with the rebels. Eventually the unrelentingly oppression would drive labor to socialism.

In the West, the indigenous rebellion against the destruction of human liberty took the form of populism. Farmers, ranchers, and communities, where they could, organized protests, formed cooperatives, and ran candidates for political office under the People's Party banner. Some of the outriders robbed banks and trains, and become folk heroes. But Populism was clumsily absorbed into the Democratic Party, and in 1899, was crucified along with William Jennings Bryan on the golden calf of the feudal capitalists. The popular McKinley was re-elected. Populism and socialism would not manage to combine their political muscle behind common interests. The Grand Old party set up to carry on its ways as always. Democracy seemed crushed head on.

At the same time, in the new urban Northeast, the Progressive Education Movement evolved, a somewhat intellectually driven, politics shy, social reform movement. The well educated upper middle class, what Lincoln and Roosevelt called silk stocking liberals, were shocked at the pitiful conditions of the foreign poor masses flocking in the factory warrens of their fair cities. This democratic impulse likewise failed to connect with the other democratic upsurges occurring throughout the nation. But in 1900, McKinley was assassinated, and Theodore Roosevelt rose to the Presidency and changed everything. What socialism, populism, and progressivism failed, was united in the person of Roosevelt.

The First Roosevelt

Both Roosevelt cousins, like the Gracchi brothers of the Roman Republic, were sons descended from the long favored upper crust families of American feudal capitalism. One would glare his peers into submission one moment, then make them feel patriotic and important the next. He would never be accepted by them. The other curried their favor, saved their positions, and would be called a traitor to his class. Theodore came first.

He was a sickly child. As part of a program to build up his physical vigor, he was set up as the don of a ranching outfit in Montana where he imbibed the cowboy culture and became intoxicated on the wide open spaces. Perhaps much of his value system was formed from this experience, though from his comments on Indians and Homesteaders, one would never suspect he would become a champion of the people. When he returned East, he went into politics as was appropriate for a person of his class, first in New York City to finally the Governorship of the State of New York. Always, he took the side the poor, the weak, and the helpless against the unjust power of landlords and corporations. He pursued reform like the army pursued Crazy Horse and became very popular with the common voters. Teddy Roosevelt, though, was too much an outrider for the Grand Old Party to trust him with its portfolio. He got slated into the Vice Presidency as the token decent politician, but that would be his peak. Then McKinley was assassinated and the Presidency fell to him. Like Jackson, he knew just what he was going to do with the power.

Roosevelt's Presidency was accompanied by two significant literary events that bolstered his cobbled together democracy. First was the publication of the *The Theory of the Leisure Class* by Thorstein Veblen, America's first original economist. In this work, Veblen debunked the presumed superiority of the robber barons, comparing them to crass barbarians that would make Attila the Hun seem civilized. He coined the phrase, "conspicuous consumption", to describe their extravagant displays of extraordinary wealth. Second was the appearance of the muckrakers, the journalists who investigated and exposed the abusive and conscienceless conduct of the unrestrained, privileged corporation. For example, they brought to light the sale of putrefying, rancid meat to the Indian Agencies and the U.S. Army. To the feudal capitalists, the soldiers and the Indians were both losers to bilk. The case for greater efforts at social reform was being well made. Roosevelt, though, went one step further. He attacked the heads of the Hydra, the trusts. Using laws passed to break up unions, he broke up the monopoly trust system, dozens at a time. Though he could only move from monopoly to oligopoly, the modicum of competition he introduced, the competition for market share, would drop prices down from monopoly levels, and would significantly increase the supply of economic goods actually produced. This action was consistent with the precepts of democratic capitalism, and was reinforced with the nation's first product liability laws.

Roosevelt turned over the Presidency to Howard Taft in 1908 in the expectation that his program of reform would be carried on. Perhaps he should have consulted his old cowboy friends who would have told him that you can never trust a fat man with power. He will be too beholden to those who feed him. Taft winked once more at obvious corruption. Roosevelt belatedly rebelled, formed a new third party, the Progressive Party, and ran again for the Presidency in 1912. He split the electorate and threw the election to Harvard born Democrat, Woodrow Wilson.

But the democratic momentum created by Teddy Roosevelt's push would lead to three new and significant democratic institutions, the independent Federal Reserve, a central banking system responsible for the money supply, the progressive income tax, modest as it was, and women's suffrage. Years later, his cousin Franklin, would use the progressive income tax to set a margin of individual wealth that would last through the Eisenhower years. This concept of a margin to individual wealth is well explained in Theodore Roosevelt's *Autobiography*.

Wilson would prove far more in love with the ideal of democracy than its actual practice. He would lead America into a European War, which Washington specifically warned against, would feed a new military industrial complex, which Eisenhower would warn against, and would consent to a viciously unjust peace in order to win his beloved League of Nations. He would repress dissent at home through laws that make the modern day Patriot Act look wishy washy. His massive contradictions would break him down during his fight to win the approval of the American Congress for his League of Nations dream. He disappeared from sight. The Grand Old Party lined up another fat man, William G. Harding, and ushered him into the White House in 1920. Wilson's ruination of democracy in order to save the world for democracy set up and lead to the Crash of 1929, the Great Depression, and World War II. Had he the nerve to support the democratic over the labor fascist faction in Russia, instead of the surviving feudal nobility, he could have prevented the Cold War. Instead of welding and developing the democratic impulses of populism, progressivism, and labor rights into a Democracy, Wilson handed the country back to the feudal capitalists.

The Second Roosevelt

Harding would die of causes natural to the obese, and turned the Presidency over to Calvin Coolidge, who rewrote the Gettysburg Address, declaring that the business of America was business. The nation of people officially became the corporate state. With its only competitor, Europe, prostrate from the devastations of war, America was the economic production capital of the world. Industrial production rose steadily throughout the twenties along with the stock market. Farmers, however, over produced and started their Great Depression early. Cheap food, which makes for cheaper subsistence wages, is a mainstay of feudal capitalism.

Meanwhile, the world, far from being made safe for democracy, had become fertile ground for reactionary extremism in the forms of communism and fascism. The production of trade goods to support the demand for American made goods faltered. The archaic colonial system squeezed the subservient dependencies to make up the difference. In the late twenties, the corporate elite, the financial upper crust, slipped the leash and began a money driven speculation that would sweep America as the faith of permanent prosperity. In early 1929, American industrial production began to slow down across the board. In the fall, the financial house of cards crashed. The slide to rock bottom took three years. By 1932, it looked as if the economy had settled into an inferior equilibrium with a permanent 20% unemployment. Plants and factories ran at 50% capacity, if at all. The banking system dissolved. Nobody wanted to borrow money, either as consumer credit or investment capital.

All this fell on the head of Herbert Hoover, who had been anointed President to follow Coolidge by the Grand Old Party, and who had won the 1928 election by a landslide. In 1932, a movie actor could have handily defeated Hoover. The Presidency fell to Franklin Delano Roosevelt, like his cousin, once Governor of New York.

If one collected all the elements of the New Deal in an abstract basket, they would represent the comprehensive program of a genuine American Democracy. But nearly all were reactions to events and conditions, rather than being the initiatives that would follow from a thoroughly thought out philosophy of democracy. Roosevelt would not develop and articulate such a philosophy until his fourth Inaugural Address, a few months before his death.

But his achievements are impressive. He put the financial markets under government regulation and oversight. Through the banking moratorium, he salvaged most of the banking system. He broke with the gold standard and devalued the dollar to prop up domestic markets. He even encouraged the industrialists to organize by sector and coordinate production to lift prices. But this smacked of national planning and was rejected out of hand. The surviving capitalists could eke by on the status quo. Any violation of their dying creed that would place their rescued privilege at risk was intolerable.

Meanwhile, Roosevelt found make work, at subsistence wages, for half of the many abandoned factory serfs, and kept they and their families alive. He gave their unions the collective bargaining power that would pay dividends for the working class in the 1950's. He introduced the blasphemous policy of agricultural subsidies that actually paid farmers and ranchers not to produce. But the control of supply supported prices that saved the family farm for the next fifty years.

In the people's interests, Roosevelt established unemployment insurance and the government run, old age pension system, though the health care plank would have to await the Great Society of Lyndon Johnson in the 1960's. Roosevelt attacked the concentration of wealth problem as thoroughly as Jackson would have done had he the position Roosevelt enjoyed. Roosevelt introduced the inheritance tax, and used high income surtaxes to set up a progressive income structure that defined a margin to individual wealth. The 95% upper bracket rate would last through the Eisenhower years. Finally, he placed a tax on corporations and introduced them to the scrutiny of the Internal Revenue Service.

But Roosevelt would never cure the Great Depression. His acts of mercy toward the many would be viewed as heresy by the surviving capitalist elite and their dependents. At a time when the economy was starved for demand, the feudal capitalist remnant passionately resisted any attempt to use their leveraged surplus to help the common others afford a livelihood. That the worker was the consumer was too much for the neanderthal brains. The apparent economic solution, to use the government budget to stimulate demand, what would become known as Keynesian economics, was published and promulgated during the 1930's. But Roosevelt's deficits would never be much more than cosmetic, never large enough to really knock the economy off its dead center, inferior equilibrium. These real stimulus would not occur until after Pearl Harbor. World War II's total mobilization would end the Great Depression, and would provide the most powerful democratic impulse among the many than had ever occurred before.

When Roosevelt at last enunciated a coherent economic and political philosophy, its refrains rang true and straight from Jefferson and Jackson's minds. His unifying theme, security, economic, political, and moral security. In his words, "We have come to the clear realization of the fact that true individual freedom cannot exist without economic security and independence." What else is freeholder status?

All citizens, without civic distinction, have a "right to a useful and remunerative job...the right to earn enough to provide adequate food and clothing and recreation; the right of every farmer to raise and sell his products at a return which will give him a decent living; the right of every businessman, large and small, to trade in an atmosphere of freedom from unfair competition and domination by monopolies…the right of every family to a decent home…to adequate medical care.. the right to adequate protection from the economic fears of old age, sickness, accident and unemployment; the right to a good education."

This Second Bill of Rights would prove a swan song. But the structural changes of Roosevelt's ad hoc democratic capitalism would produce the Golden Age of the American Middle Class. Dwight D. Eisenhower, from Kansas, the first and last moderate Republican President, would preside over the climax of the fitful waves of democracy that accompanied the coincidental rise to power of the Roosevelt cousins.

The Eisenhower Tide

Normally, any socio-historical phenomena that puts many people in motion, and brings them into frequent communication with others outside their home grown circles, breeds grassroots, democratic sentiments. The Great Depression began this. Many found themselves in the streets together, standing in lines to find work or get a bowl of soup. Others roamed the country hitching rides on the rails in search of opportunity. World War II carried on this leveling like a second flood. Tens of millions were mobilized for the war effort, men into uniforms, women into the factories. Suddenly there was a paycheck for everybody, and one better than any had for all the depressing years earlier. Factories zoomed to 100% production. New industrial plant and equipment were constructed as fast as possible. Even with consumer rationing, households enjoyed a standard of living sufficient and pleasant when compared to what the Great Depression had provided. This primary, conditioning reality operated for three and a half years. The War would also produce a military hero like none since Jackson, one who could command on both fields, civilian and military.

There would be no return to any illusions of normalcy. The madness of Stalin, the atomic bomb, Joseph McCarthy, and the Korean War, would create a new Cold War Terror. But the soldiers came home, married the girls, took their place in the factories, sired the largest native born generation of new Americans to date, and found they had collective bargaining power. Through its exercise, the once and recently downtrodden working class moved into the middle class. With Keynesian fiscal policy at its disposal, the government committed itself to a full employment economy. Roosevelt's margin to individual wealth still held, 95% in the top bracket. A modern, majority, middle class democracy enjoyed a natural birth, partly because of historical forces, but just as surely, because of the deep structural changes created in American Society brought about by the Jefferson, Jackson, and the ad hoc Roosevelts Democracies.

Eisenhower would keep this in tact. He would stand off the foreign threats and ease the economy through two mild inventory recessions, creating the foreign and domestic peace that would give courage to the civil rights movements. He would build the Interstate highway system and produce more American mobility and communication then ever before. In his last address to the nation he would desparately warn the people about the unnatural power and influence of Cold War's growing military industrial complex, the national security conglomerations of corporations feeding off the federal budget. Eisenhower possessed the same strength of personal character that Jackson possessed. He defined just moderation in all things. He is the grandfather of the American Middle Class, and deserves his place as the third great name in the Long Night of American Democracy, when democratic progress was circumstantial instead of proactive. One of his early moves, and perhaps most structural, was the appointment of Earl Warren as Chief Justice of the Supreme Court. After centuries of religiously observing the old federalist faith, the Supreme Court would look to advance democracy. In 1954, the Warren Court ruled that separate, but equal, schools were unconstitutional. Blacks, and all the left out rest, would now be integrated and diversified into mainstream American society.

This last wave of American Democracy would culminate in the 1960's with the Civil Rights Legislation and the socialization of health care for the poor and elderly. But the stresses and tensions that the new world order of globally integrating systems of politics, economies, and cultures, would spawn cast dark shadows over the emerging triumph of democracy. The Viet Nam War and civil rights discord would divide the nation. The oil cartel of the 1970's and the Japanese made automobile would break the trance. No natural leaders emerged. Crisis followed crisis as the media grew into its current attention deficit syndrome of chronic hysteria. The time was ripe for the counter revolution.

The Empire Strikes Back

It was surely inevitable in a celebrity worshiping pop culture that a Grade B actor with a winning smile would be rescued from oblivion to lead the Grand Old

Party Revival. In the 1950's, Ronald Reagan was well paid, well enough to mingle with those to the manner born, for giving a series of ghost written, political speeches and lectures in the ideology that would become known as Conservatism. He learned his lines well. He reached out to those who would gladly rule America as a theocracy, the socio-religious fundamentalists, and became their prophet to lead them from out of the wilderness. The puritans and the patricians made common cause. The formula worked first in California, where he became Governor, and finally, nationally, when he ascended to the Presidency in 1980, destroying what was left of the Eisenhower Moderation. Reagan's Presidency marks the beginning of the latter day feudal reaction to the democratic progress thus far achieved in the 20th century.

Though the cobbled together planks of intellectual, conservative ideology lack the deep structural coherence and candor of Hamilton's federalist vision, the goals of its policies are the same. A major difference between the two ideologies concerns to role of government. Hamilton wanted a strong government to righteously divide society into what he believed were its two natural parts, the few and the many. But Jackson proved that strong government in the hands of democracy was a bad idea. What one wanted was a government strong enough to send in the troops at the bidding of the capitalist lords, yet otherwise content itself with committee meetings and dinner parties. The Robber Barons had this, on a permanent basis, within their grasp in 1899 and 1929, but the democratic winds arising from the Frontier West, the Great Depression, and World War II, guided through the leadership of the the Roosevelts and Eisenhower, unsettled all that. Government for the people was strong again and working on their behalf, trying to create one people instead of two, an undivided, free society instead of a divided hierarchical society.

Now back in power, the disciples of Conservatism would bend government to their will, exploit all they could on behalf of their class. Then, destroying the castle from within, enfeeble it to the point of impotency. To prevent it from ever being strong again in the hands of democracy forever.

Through vigorous deregulation and through feeding regulatory agencies starvation budgets, the restraints needed to enforce democratic capitalism were loosened and ignored. Corporate business went on a looting campaign. The savings and loan banking system sector, organized like populist cooperatives, were liquidated. But individual investors were insured up to $100,000 by the government so the government paid the looting bill, some 300 billion dollars worth. The military industrial complex not only rang up record budget deficits finally pounding the Soviet Union into insolvency, it gouged another 300 billion in Star Wars spending. Through massive tax cuts, the national debt soared, and the individual margin to individual wealth contained in the progressive tax structure was replaced with a flat tax. Capital money was granted special favored status. Capital gains income and dividend income are now taxed at lower rates than regular, job income, creating an overtly regressive tax structure as clearly favoring a privileged elite as the feudal tax laws favored Europe's 15th century aristocracy. The rich do not simply stay rich, they get richer, and the poor make up the difference. The middle class flattens out and divides into those going up and those going down. Unions are busted, cowed into submission, or bought off. In the late '80's, corporate earnings swelled. The stock market boomed, then crashed with the Berlin Wall, recovered, and boomed again until the World Trade Center Towers fell. The multinational corporations grew into unregulated giants with budgets and power greater than most sovereign nations. American jobs were pooled with the cheaper labor of the Third World and were sent there, replaced at home with more service sectors jobs. The demand for domestic servants invites illegal immigration. The opposition party, by doting on enhancing the civil rights of various ethnically defined voter constituency segments, reinforce the often racially driven strategy of dividing the many into feuding petty classes, too conditioned to exclusive attitudes toward strangers to find common cause. Bread and circuses lull the masses, while in the name of patriotic war, dissent is hunted down and privacy invaded with all the vigor of John Adams.

This is the present. Congress outlaws competition in prescription drugs. Regulations are gutted and special favors are granted without shame at will. An Alabama judge puts a stone monument of the Ten Commandments on court-house premises. The Higher Courts make him remove this blatant violation of the separation between religion and state. But no one thinks to move the sculpture to the sidewalks of Wall Street where it might do some good. The insider business there has never been so good, especially the insider business with government. The corporate state for itself is back. The prize is once again within the grasp of Hamilton's ghost.

Perchance To Dream

As the 21st century opens, American Democracy is more of a wraith than a tangible presence. Conservatism has named its opposition, its nemesis, Liberalism, but there is no deep ideological unity to this creature, only a conglomeration of popular, but narrow interest groups, largely ethnic, gender, or environment related. The so called Democratic Party seems more entangled in liberalism's polyglot web than leading and shaping it. Certainly the great aims and issues of American Democracies from the past are feared, ignored, or neglected.

One could wonder what thoughts, principles, and convictions would move across King Arthur's Round Table were Jefferson, Jackson, Lincoln, Teddy, Dwight, and Franklin convened there to size up the situation, and the needed, necessary strategies to save the nation of a people for the people, and chances of progress such liberty promises. Like a Higher Court of Human Liberty. Were a full scale, full court press American Democracy to unfold now, what would it look like? The four theaters of campaign are political democracy, the distribution of wealth, democratic capitalism, and the culture of freedom.

Political Democracy

The only political security a democracy has lies in the popular vote. Unless the many can discover their common interests, and combine in electoral majorities, no chance of equal rights and opportunities will be possible. Even with the popular vote, democratic liberty is always a difficult progress. The Popular Will must have the means to decisively express itself. Otherwise democracy is a mirage of theory and myth.

A nation of people dedicated to democracy will invest in the best voter registration and recording technology possible. As the first order of business for each fiscal year, the governmental entities of a political democracy should fund a public election budget, one designed to properly support qualifying candidates, and thus promote political competition. What is good for the markets in good and services is also good for the suffrage market.

The persistent trend in sub 40% voter turnout is a national disgrace. In the corporate world, such percentages would be termed mere minority interests. Some countries require a 50% vote to validate its elections. America should vastly exceed that number as a matter of patriotic pride. There is no reason for the polling period to last only a day. Why not three days? The practice of suffrage is the most important thing that we do. The pro forma media hysteria, trying to call the result first as breaking news, will soon exhaust itself. We can wait three days to learn the Popular Will. Anything less than 50% is only minority government, ideal for expropriation by those reviving the Hamilton tradition.

An equal shame is the corrupting influence of money, of wealth, on election campaigns, and the subsequent conduct of the politicians so beholden. The government should keep its money out of business, and business should keep its money out government. Campaign finance laws and the public election budgets should keep such bribery and blackmail combinations in the back room and not in the Congressional Record. To qualify for public welfare, the citizen must prove irredeemable poverty. Corporate welfare should only go to the corporations that can prove bankruptcy.

The two party system is also defective. It is more stable than the multiparty coalitions of parliamentary government, but lacks its room for political evolution. In the current political balance between the so called Democratic and Republican Parties, a bloc of voters, independents, decides most elections. Being uncommitted to party pledges, they vote as they choose, for reasons of their own. Were voter turnouts to approach 60%, this Independent Party would grow, while the two minority parties would shrink, leaving room for a third minority party, call them the Reform Party, the Liberal Party, or the Whigs. The Independents, the freeholders of political democracy, will have more choices, and the increased competition will stimulate the development of political leadership.

Also, a political democracy would revive no strings attached, revenue sharing between local, state, and federal governments. Such a return of taxes to their point of origin balances the distribution of burden with direct, return benefits, thus stabilizing governmental operations from local to national levels. The fact and idea that the national government should be free to run enormous deficits while states drastically cut spending and services is unacceptable.

Finally, government secrecy and political democracy are incompatible. The citizen, through the rights of privacy, has greater rights to secrecy as suits them than does the government, at any level. The government has no right to privacy. It has no inherent right to secrecy supposedly for the good of the people. It is up to the people to decide. Some say that the unidentified flying object scandals and coverups are motivated by a desire to protect the people of the world from the truth. What folly that would prove should galactic pirates akin to the British Empire to show up and take all five billion of us down, unawares, because we were in no way prepared, mentally, emotionally, and physically, to resist as a people, a single human species. Truth and freedom are inseparable.

The other touted motive for government secrecy is national security. This logically leaves out state and local government. Yet we do, as a common people, understand the need that some decisions, communications, and activities, done in our name, need secrecy to be effective. But the long running, often hysterical, Cold War created a gargantuan, obsessive appetite for classifying the business of government as secretive matters. It seems that neither the people, or freedom, can be trusted with the truth. In the long run, all government secrets must become society's public property. Allowing the grace of death to pass first should be the only exception.

The Distribution of Wealth

Lasting concentrations of wealth are incompatible with democracy. The goal is to achieve the most normally distributed distribution of wealth possible. The more the wealth is piled up in the middle, the stronger the democracy.

Therefore, any regressive income tax scheme, whether indirect as the flat tax, or direct as the free dividends no tax, will, by necessary structure, cause the rich to become richer, and the poor poorer, such a scheme is unacceptable. That the rich are rich should be enough. The burdens of the poor should likewise be severe enough. A significantly upward sweeping progressive tax structure, containing a 95% margin to individual wealth, must be installed again. The high ground must be retaken.

In defining income, the rule should be that any and all income is income, whether gained by sweat, guile, capital gains, interest, or dividend, and should be taxed at the same rate. What else could be fairer? In the same vein, any and all property is property. If property in the form of land and housing is taxed, so should other forms of net worth.

There are two goals to distribution of wealth policy, to keep it liquid and circulating, and to keep it piled up in the middle, that is, normatively distributed. The prospects of the third and fourth generation heirs of the nouveau riche and the present poor should be roughly the same.

As for the normative distribution of wealth, it possess four justifications: 1) It is morally just; 2) It promotes political comity; 3) It nurtures a healthier society. Psychological research has shown that prejudice, bigotry, and social antagonisms are reduced, and tolerance increased, through contact and communication with individuals of the vilified class; and 4) It promotes stability in economic production. Producing millions of washing machines for a majority middle class is inherently, even statistically, more stable then building hundreds of yachts and mansions for the megarich.

Democratic Capitalism

The general goals of democratic capitalism are to harness the money driven production system so that it serves society instead of capturing it, and to see that the benefits of economic performance are evenly distributed to those holding an interest in the performance of the economy, namely, the people of the nation.

Point one. This means that the competitive, free enterprise system must be rigorously maintained and strengthened, and thoroughly policed for corruption and combinations of unequal power, the capitalist mafiosa. Monopolies, not required by infrastructure demands, should be broken up on principle, if not for price and quality improvements, for the inherent innovative stimulus competition provides. Oligopic combinations must be prevented from increasing their concentrations for the same reasons. Over the long run, massive woolly corporate behemoths will fail, leaving the sector bereft of working productive capacity.

But the multinational corporation, with global operations, presents a more serious problem. Not only do these creatures have little regard for their employees when cutting costs, they have little regard for the nations in which they operate if they can leverage their interests through the power of wealth. They have no international scrutiny or regulation. They seem obligated to no country or people. They send the people's livelihood, their jobs, to overpopulated countries, where a big bowl of rice a day is a living wage. They overpower marginal third world governments with money and gratuitous largess, then execute lucrative natural resource extraction contracts, like at Gold Ridge on Guadalcanal of the Solomon Islands. A united nations institution is needed to hold these global entities accountable for their conduct before a court of world standing.

Point two. Management of the nation's money supply must be kept incorruptible. While the performance of the Federal Reserve System at the end of the 20th century has been remarkably effective, it success is largely because it has kept the money supply proportional to the volume of trade needing money for a medium of exchange. Not for other reasons. Stimulative manipulations of the money supply are risky, and should be used only as a last resort, after fiscal policy, or the natural recuperative properties of competitive capitalism, have failed.

But the high priests of finance are too easily susceptible to the prayers of their practitioners. After the Towers Fell, Wall Street begged the Federal Reserve for liquidity, meaning credit, to stop the stock market crash that followed. The obliging creation of excess money has propped up the stock market to a moving average just above or below 10,000, and is currently being palmed off on the world as a devalued dollar. Had the Federal Reserve stayed with production proportionality, all the air in the market's speculation bubble would have dissipated, and the current economic recovery would still be modestly underway, the dollar strong. Better the Federal Reserve's Board of Directors lived and dined in Denver.

Point three. The worker is the consumer. Job worker income is consumer demand. This business of multinational corporations shipping American jobs overseas to cheap labor cesspools, and then importing back cheap goods is like sacrificing your children for an extra turkey at Christmas. Or like the Spanish conquistadors shipping off the New World gold to the European ruling classes, leaving only a hole in the ground. Neither religion, social justice, or native conscience, has prevented the feudal society minded from treating their workers like less deserving lackeys needing only a minimum standard of living. The working class is the backbone of the middle class, and its position there must be assured and reinforced.

Consequently, the Social Contract must be rewritten. Labor brings its own capital interest to economic enterprise. In the event of economic profits, labor should be paid worker dividends in the same position as the preferred stockholder. Such a sharing of the profit streams of production would cause a more normative distribution of remuneration within the collective enterprise, and would assure labor a solid place in the middle class. Such a scheme might trim the sails of the managerial and capitalist classes, but would hardly prostrate them. Again the worker who makes the product is the consumer who buys the product en masse.

But the most pressing problem is how do we bring the jobs back to America. Or does the American worker have no better future than that of obsequious servantry, like the servant class that coddled European aristocracy?

Point four. Centralized government should be small, but strong. Small because local and state government should be able to handle most of the governance needs of the people. And strong because a democracy cannot survive a prolonged weak and enfeebled government, while an exclusive, well endowed ruling class thrives on such.

Point five, Democratic capitalism will favor small business of over big business, and protect manufacturing business from the predations of financial business.

Point six. A permanent national debt is unacceptable. Its relatively marginal percentages of the total national output are irrelevant. The federal budget should have room to effectively carry out countervailing fiscal policy. The $400 billion annual interest payment is deadweight loss to the nation. One single matching appropriation would revitalize the entire American steel industry. Not to mention that the national debt creates the easy sinecures desired by Hamilton's privileged aristocracy.

Point seven. In strict terms, democratic capitalism would keep government money out of business, and business money out of government. Corporate welfare, either to subsidize business investment and activity that it should do in its own right, or to make profitable unprofitable enterprises, makes no economic sense. Should bonanza type profits result, what share does the government get for its help? The current haphazard looting should be formalized into national planning. That way there is some chance that long run benefits might accrue to the people. For example, move the steel industry out of the World War I era to the 21st century. Or better, manufacture the plastic I-beam, which science has already shown to be lighter, stronger, and more resistant to degradation than the metallic version.

The Culture of Freedom

First and foremost, freedom and liberty can only grow where the rights of privacy are protected. Privacy rights stand in the same relation to the person as do property rights, and should be equally protected. A culture of freedom must be libertarian biased. Provided no unnatural harm comes to others, people should be free to ruin, or exalt, their lives as God gives them leave to.

The whole point of these reforms in political democracy, the distribution of wealth, and democratic capitalism, is to create the optimum conditions of human liberty, the free society, thus assuring that the future of society, its grandchildren, will enjoy mobility, social justice, common decency, and material progress. But as the Golden Rule is better known than practiced, so, too, we seem to extoll freedom while fearing to give it reign. We run constantly to the government to micromanage our petty fears and prejudices upon others who we cannot personally convince, or perhaps not even care about. A culture of freedom must be persistently libertarian. If no harm falls to others, leave the citizen alone.

If one had to reduce the essence of human liberty and the free society to two general policies, one could do no better than these. To trust freedom. And observe the Golden Rule. Not only do unto thy neighbor what you would have done for yourself, but do business with others as you would have business done with yourself.

Only then will we find out if the human being, human culture, is worth all the trouble.

A Short List of the Great Documents of American Democracy

The Preamble to the Declaration of Independence

The Preamble to the United States Constitution

The Bill of Rights, the First Ten Amendments

The Bank Veto Message to Congress

Jackson's Farewell Address

Henry David Thoreau's On Civil Disobedience

The Gettysburg Address

Franklin Roosevelt's Last Inaugural Speech

Martin Luther King's Letter from Birmingham Jail

REPRESENTATIVE SOURCES

Stone Age Economics, Marshall Sahlins, Aldine De Gruyter, New York, 1972.

The Story of Civilization, Volumes I to XI, Will and Ariel Durant, Simon and Schuster, New York, 1935 to 1975.

The Celts, the People who Came Out of Darkness, Gerhard Herm, St. Martin's Press, New York, 1975.

A People's History of the United States, 1492–Present, Howard Zinn, Harper Collins, New York, 1995.

The Virginia Adventure: Roanoke to James Towne: an Archaelogical and Historical Odysssey, Ivor Noel Hume, Knoft, New York, 1994.

How the Scots Invented the Modern World: The True Story of How Western Europe's Poorest Nation Created Our World and Everything in It, Arthur Herman, Crown Publishers, New York, 2001.

The Age of Jackson, Arthur Schlesinger, Jr., Little Brown, New York, 1945.

Teachings from the Worldly Philosophy, Robert Heilbroner, W. W. Norton & Company, New York, 1996

Douglas Southall Freeman's *Washington*

Carl Sandburg's *Lincoln*

Theodore Roosevelt's *Autobiography*

William Manchester's *The Glory and the Dream*

Anything by *John Kenneth Galbraith*

Notes Concerning the Measurement of Wealth and the
Consequences of the Assumed Scale and its Properties on the Long Run
Distribution or Maldistribution of Real Wealth Within a Population

Raven Walker

"It is to be regretted, that the rich and powerful too often bend the acts of government to their selfish purposes.

Distinctions in society will always exist under every just government. Equality of talents, of education, or of wealth cannot be produced by human institutions. In the full enjoyment of the gifts of Heaven and the fruits of superior industry, economy, and virtue every man is equally entitled to protection by law; but when the laws undertake to add to these natural and just advantages artificial distinction...to make the rich richer and the potent more powerful, the humble members of society—the farmers, mechanics, and laborers—who have neither the time nor the means of securing like favors to themselves, have a right to complain of the injustice of their Government.

Its evils exist only in its abuses. If it would confine itself to equal protection, and...shower its favors alike on the high and low, the rich and the poor, it would be an unqualified blessing. In the act before me, there seems to be a wide and unnecessary departure from these just principles.

Its vast power, concentrated in the hands of a few men irresponsible to the people, will be a constant threat to the American future."

From Andrew Jackson's Message to Congress
Explaining his Veto Against the Rechartering of the Bank of the United States.

1   If the rich merely remained rich, and the poor only stayed poor, an unequal distribution of real wealth would acquire the sanctity of long custom. But with maldistribution, the rich get richer, and the poor poorer, until the social fabric breaks down. In maldistributive societies, the rich are able to buy and consume an increasingly larger proportion of the real wealth produced by the economy, while the proportion allotted the poor shrinks. To provide for this, larger numbers of the population, in fact, become poorer.

One of the commodities the moneyed rich can buy in greater proportion is power. They use this advantage to maintain the status quo which assures their pre-eminent position, if not improve it.

2   All phenomena are naturally qualitative in direct experience. Their quantitative nature we infer and surmise. We introduce quantity in our effort to describe and analyze the phenomena. We measure aspects and properties of the phenomena, and use quantitative analysis, and symbolic, functional formulations, to identify correlations between the qualitative behavior of the phenomena, finding recurrent, reliable behavior in the numbers measured on our assumed number scale, and therefore, in the theoretical variables we use to formulate our relational quantitative description. So are found the laws of science.

3   Wealth is a human phenomena. Only when, through the superior human intelligence, cunning, and language, we garner a distinguishable share of provision above what the animals manage does anything thing like wealth matter. But when we secure such surplus for real, how we conceive wealth, and measure and distribute it, matters a great deal. No ancient civilization solved the problem of the distribution of wealth. All fell when the maldistribution of wealth became so severe not even animals could withstand it.

4   The production, accumulation, and use of wealth is, in effect, our manifest material standard of living. This phenomena is clearly susceptible to quantitative analysis. We all keenly notice the more or less, the have and the have not. It all begins with food. We can observe the distribution and consumption of food wealth in the population in waistlines, and measure the individual differences with a tape measure or a bathroom scale. Serious divergencies can be easily identified by using the statistical laws of probability theory. Height, weight, waistline are all normally distributed. Abnormal trends then are detected objectively. Americans are the fattest population on earth.

Ethiopians are the skinniest. With the effect observed, the cause can be sought. In this example, obviously the Americans are the most well fed, and the Ethiopians the most often famine stricken.

Accounting for real wealth, and its individual differences, is the business of measurement, mathematics, and theoretical formulations. The first decision is with respect to the scale of measurement. Is it nominal, ordinal, interval, or cardinal? Since one can observe the occurrence of no wealth, or nearest thing next to, wealth is cardinal. One can have some and one can have none.

5   Cardinal scales are themselves dividable into two kinds. Mathematically, they can be limited to arithmetic operations, or expandable through geometric or exponential operations. Arithmetic phenomena and their corresponding scales will be normally distributed. Geometric phenomena and their corresponding scales will be lognormally distributed. The second critical decision concerns whether the phenomena is arithmetic or geometric in its actual nature.

6   The question is, is the nature of the wealth arithmetic or geometric?

Examples of phenomena of a geometric nature are gravity, electromagnetic propagation, and population reproduction. To mathematically describe their behavior geometric functions are necessary, such as the inverse square law.

The measurement of earthquakes is also a geometric phenomena. The actual raw data measuring the disturbances in the earth are so consistently geometric in expansion that it is necessary to apply a logarithmic correction to make the scale interpretatively sensible. Thus on the Richter Scale, one interval represents a ten fold increase in the numerical content of the raw data.

Velocity, on the other hand, is arithmetic, or linear, in nature. It remains constant unless subject to some force causing acceleration. But even this multiplier is arithmetic in increase, constant in magnitude and independent of changes in the base velocity. Acceleration will cause a brief geometric episode of increase, but once removed, velocity becomes stable once more.

Digging a hole in the ground is likewise arithmetic. One removes a shovel full at a time, from moment to moment. The shovel full remains constant in magnitude. Through application of technology, the dirt produced can undergo a leap in yield that create a brief episode of geometric expansion. But once the technology has had its immediate effects, the yield becomes stable again. The increase in excavation does not expand as the hole becomes deeper. Increases are only possible by improvement in technology, and are of a specific magnitude. The shovel full does not increase, though the mass of the dirt removed increases, a shovel full at a time, from moment to moment.

7 Height, weight, and age are also arithmetic phenomena. They are normally distributed within the population. So is food production. Wealth measured in potatoes and pigs is arithmetic. If you double your acres, you double your yield. You do not quadruple your yield. Accordingly, such phenomena prove normally distributed. Sample all the fields of like size in a county, distribute their yields, and one gets the bell curve. Double your leavings, and the field mice increase geometrically. Double your free food on the ground, and four times as many mice will ferociously compete for it.

8 Both with farm and factory production, yield or output is not added back to the original base. For the farmer, the base is land. For the factory owner, the base is the fixed assets. One can add land or fixed assets, but if otherwise constant, yield or output increases only as technology improves.

9 What distinguishes the geometric increase from the arithmetic increase is that the geometric increase is added back into the base, thereby causing the next increase to expand, that is, become larger without any change in conditions except for that addition. An arithmetic increase is simply a moment to moment increase of a specific magnitude. The shovel full itself does not increase.

10 Phenomena of fundamentally arithmetic nature can undergo observable geometric expansion, in particular, with phenomena distributed over time. First occurrences appear infrequently, then the rate of increase over time increases until a pivot point is met. Then the rate of increases decreases until it levels off, or falls. This kind of phenomena is described by the normal O-Jive curve, a correlative function of the normal distribution theory of probability. Equilibrium sets in.

For example, skyscrapers. The first built made clear that many more would be a profitable net. So cities vied to erect their own first, then more, until all the prime space for skyscrapers is located, bought up, and built. For a while, the rate of increase over time will accelerate, then slow, and finally stall. Now skyscrapers still go up, but many go down, demolished to make room for newer and bigger skyscrapers.

The physical limit causes the final arithmetic equilibrium. A skyscraper will not be built in a wheat field of western Kansas. Without the real, natural limit, the expansion could continue unabated. Skyscrapers would already be crowding out the wheat fields in western Kansas.

11   Ordinarily, this first question of whether the nature of the phenomena is arithmetic or geometric is only a problem in measurement and mathematical expression. One refines the conceptual kit empirically by pitting it against more observations, discarding those methods and ideas that fail to describe and predict. But in some instances, as in economy, the scales of measurement employed become, in effect, tools, causative factors in managing and affecting the phenomena itself. Then the issue passes from pure science to policy. In the case of wealth, the measure is money, on some arbitrary scale of currency.

12   Ordinarily, one does not expect the scale of measure for a phenomena to possess a dynamic life of its own. It makes no sense to think of the scale of pounds or inches increasing. The phenomena varies, not the scale. The scale is simply an analogical device applied objectively to factual properties of the phenomena to obtain a quantitative description of the behavior of those properties measured.

Money, on the other hand, in addition to providing a scale with which wealth is measured, possesses dynamic phenomenological properties of its own. It increases or decreases independently of increases in the real wealth it measures. Taken as concrete, hard currency, money is subject to the iron laws of economic production in an environment of scarce resources, just like any other material good. To make a gold coin, one must find and dig gold.

Taken in the abstract, through the mathematical device of the interest rate, money can increase without such physical constraint. Money increases, by the theory of interest and the faith of loans, and in that theory, possesses no real limit except as its function as a medium of exchange fails or succeeds. In the concrete sense, money is arithmetic in nature. In the abstract sense, money is geometric in nature. As money is free to vary without significant reference to real wealth, as a phenomena in its own right, distortions i distribution become possible that otherwise would have never existed.

13 A curious, global, empirical trend can be found in the diggings by archeologists through the many layers of dwellings in the ancient towns and cities of humankind. Taking dwelling space as a measure of wealth, many living spaces might be 10x10, and a near number, 14x14. Numerically, this is an area difference of roughly 2 to 1. But how many humans can occupy that space? Without use, wealth is meaningless. If ten can stand 100 square feet, can twenty stand only 200 square feet? Both human need and the consumption of real wealth are arithmetic phenomena. If ten can be abide a 100 square feet, ten living in 1,000 have gained disportionately.

Take this observable, archeological evidence of the natural inequality among humans as the norm for the natural tolerance of an unequal distribution of the wealth. Later layers of the city show growing divergencies. Ten foot walls become twenty foot walls, four times the lower class space. Finally palaces and mansions appear, with stacked cubical tenements to house the throngs still living in the 10x10 space. Or less. Always on the edge of dispossession.

14 As it develops out of barter, money is first concrete. As the civilization and its economy become increasingly complex, money becomes more and more abstract and mathematical in its application. The capacity to create money without the production constraints of scarce resources is discovered, along with its seductive benefits and pitfalls, the stimulation of economic activity, the possibility of geometrically expanding shares of the wealth, inflation, and the capacity for severe, sudden reductions after speculation episodes, fueled by the generous increase in the money supply, collapse.

The speculative episodes are possible only because the money supply has separated from its referent, real wealth. You cannot bid up prices beyond all rationality without large excesses of money available. Speculative episodes are, in fact, defined by geometric expansions of money, thought to be and held as a substitute for real wealth. The lack of reality is invariably confirmed by the collapse of the bubble and the geometric evaporation of the same money.

15 Instead of falling into a long run, entrenching pattern following the first lines of the merely natural inequality in the distribution of wealth, an arithmetic phenomena, wealth becomes maldistributed. By geometric expansion, the well to do become the rich, the rich get richer, and the poor pay for this. The poor live just as primally as ever, while the rich live like one once thought only the gods, or kings, could live.

A far higher percentage of what wealth the poor and working class garner goes to securing the base material necessaries than is spent by the rich. By base necessaries assume some quasi floating standard of comfortability. Granted one does not expect the very well off to live as the poor, but if the poor think $20,000 a year secured as swimming with their heads above water, obviously a millionaire is running at a 90% luxury surplus. When the rich get richer, their surplus starts to run around 900%. Invariably, the base proportion of the poor diminishes to accommodate this expansion of wealth and purchasing power acquired by the rich without lifting a finger. The rich get richer. And the poor get poorer, most often, in the most abundant and affluent of times, when one would think that natural inequalities would be reduced through the will of religion.

What causes this?

16 The most notable instance of an analysis of human and economic phenomena having divergent quantitative natures is Malthus' study of the rates of food production and population reproduction, and the necessary consequences of the divergent natures. Food production increases arithmetically, if it increases at all. Population expands geometrically, consuming any surplus with the net long run effect of reducing per capita consumption back to its original subsistence levels. But only after positive checks are administered by Nature, dramatic subtractions from overpopulation, such as famine, war, and disease, remove the population surplus created by the geometric expansion to restore a sustainable equilibrium between the two phenomena, producing food and reproducing population.

Numerous writers of contemporary fame since have belittled the dire predictions Malthus's analysis portends. Wonderful advances in agrarian technologies have pushed the increase in food production to the fullest sail of its arithmetic, limited nature. But the inevitable nature of the problem is unchanged. One cannot cheat Malthus, only defer his consequences. Even now, world food production is falling while population is burgeoning toward unbelievable magnitudes. Doubters of Thomas should go live in Bangladesh for one year. The iron law of wealth and supply cannot be evaded. Real wealth, be it food or other material things, can only be produced. Scarce resources constrain such production to arithmetic behavior. Double the yield of the rice paddies in Bangladesh for ten years, and the population enjoying such providence will quadruple. But soon the doubled yield becomes stable, while all the increase in population are added to the base, therefore set to expand geometrically in the next moment of generation. Mouths are bound to go empty.

17 The only cure is to establish a population equilibrium within the limits of food production, and therefore, sustainable over the long run without the disagreeable application of positive checks. Human society has continually failed this goal, this test. The longer such sustainable equilibrium is put off or deferred by technology and the aggressive exploitation of natural resources, the more catastrophic the eventual collapse of the artificial edifice will be. As they say, the taller the tree, the harder it falls.

18 Self evidently, wealth is measurable on arithmetic scales, palatably enough to understand the physical difference, bushels and pounds of food and flesh, square footage, or by the sheer counting off of units of material things possessed. But wealth is also measured in money, the exchange value relationship between wealth phenomena and the record keeping scale of this thing called money, the arbitrary medium of exchange.

But because money is a phenomena in its own right, one can hold wealth as money, as a store of wealth, and as a temporary substitute for wealth. If the quantitative nature of money is different from the quantitative nature of real wealth, then each will prove subject to different, independently motivated mathematical laws of increase. If money can increase geometrically while real wealth can increase only arithmetically, then over the long run, the holders of money will acquire a significant increase in purchasing power over the holders of mere real wealth. The holders of money will crowd out the holders of land and fixed assets because they can increase their base through the assessments of interest.

19 In pure abstraction, the scale of money is without limit. Through manipulations like compound interest, money can increase from a small-in-magnitude base to one of astronomical size in a lifetime. The key is that the increase is added to the base. Mathematical money, as presently created, is explosively geometric, without external limits. This is the compounding effect. This effect is considered justified as the reward for deferred consumption. If 50 liberally covers base necessaries, and two persons make 50 each period, were one to consume only 30, and hold the rest as money, the future funded nicely offsets the present sacrifice. But if one makes 100, and holds the excess over base necessaries as a substitute for real wealth, money, then the ratio between

the two persons moves from 2:1 through 3:1 on to 4:1. At 4 to 1, the one can seriously start outbidding the other for the best of the necessaries, and buy luxury wholly beyond what the other can manage holding at a steady 50 as periodic income.

Increases in arithmetic phenomena are not added to the base. One can take 100 acres, and through improved technology, increase the yield some percentage of past yields. But the increase cannot be added to the base. One can step to a new level, but without further advances in technology, the gain stays the same in sheer magnitude, year after year.

20 The reason food and material wealth are arithmetic in nature is because food and other forms of real wealth must be produced from scarce resources. There is no way biomass and its conversion can geometrically expand when the critical resources, soil, water, and minerals, are severely limited from the outset.

Money, on the other hand, is created out of money, with no a priori limit. At one time, when money was a concrete phenomena, limited by fixed ties to some natural resource such as precious metal, at a time when mathematics was still largely refinements of arithmetic, what passed as money, hard currency, was accordingly arithmetic in nature. The magnitudes between real wealth and money might be all out of whack, but the basic underlying scales were the same. When proportionality is achieved, economic activity becomes stable. This is clearly why the Gold Standard survived so long. Without such a link to a real resource, money becomes totally abstract, and consequently, its geometric nature is allowed relatively free reign to express itself.

When money is restricted by a resource limit, its store of value function is constrained to a real arithmetic nature. When money is restricted by rates and capital reserve requirements, confinement to arithmetic bounds is suspended, and its rate of increase subject only to law and custom. When such feeble chains are removed, money multiplies like the rabbits in Australia. One of the first things money buys up is the power to sustain and improve its position.

21 Monetarist theory provides such tools of theory, law, and custom, and places the mechanisms of such control in the central banking system. Even then it is a double edged sword, and somewhat tardy in its effects. By implication, however, money now ceases to be a mere measure of wealth, once proportionately indistinguishable from real wealth, and becomes a phenomena in its

own right subject to manipulation, for the purpose of manipulating the macro economic world.

22 A new factor is introduced when money takes on a phenomenological life of its own. Because we wish to use the concept of money to store value as a substitute for real wealth where the purchasing power held in ready abeyance, we incorporate the geometric scale of measurement literally. When both real wealth and money are constrained to arithmetic natures, both poor and rich can make proportional draws and maintain an equilibrium. That is, the rich do not become richer, and the poor do not become poorer. When the rich become richer and the poor poorer, maldistribution is occurring. The accounting for wealth becomes warped and distorted. The geometric properties of the monetary scale are the cause.

Any distribution of the real wealth exposed to geometric expansion will become a maldistribution, inequities appearing far beyond the inequalities of distribution natural to real wealth, the normally distributed inequality based upon ability, ambition, and chance.

The maldistribution of wealth has serious social consequences, oftentimes destroying those who benefit most from, and seek to maintain, the same maldistribution, even conspiring to increase it. The rich, in a maldistributed society, are usually outnumbered 100 to 1, or better. Taking the global perspective, with 80 to 90 per cent of the total population in the lower middle class and below, the numbers match the French Revolution. Only religious dogma, pure power, full control of the police state, and long revered custom, can maintain such maldistribution. And after a certain point, even this fails.

23 When real wealth is possessed as money, and that money can be geometrically expanded while in possession, the cumulative aggregate amount can then be used to buy an even greater proportion of real wealth then was originally possessed. A person possessing real wealth as real wealth has no leverage against this individual possessing the monetary process of wealth acceleration. How else could the rich get richer and the poor poorer, without such automatic and artificial distortion? The rich sit on their money and gain, and the poor sit on their real wealth and lose.

When practiced on a collective scale, the possessors of money and its geometric expansion are able to acquire an increasing share of the real wealth. Exactly what is going on is pure empirical fact and well measured. The distribution of wealth is skewing. But only at the expense of someone else, the less moneyed, or of no money at all, namely labor. Labor, which now must compete with the billions of mass poor the third world has spawned, slides downward. Imagine how the rich would respond to having to live and work as the common man. How many would gladly be willing to give up half their wealth to avoid it.

24 For labor, mere holders of real wealth, money has only the convenience of exchange. Their labor is exchanged for money just enough to trade for necessities and a few discretionary items, month by month. Indeed, by the device of the mortgage, while making home ownership possible, also succeeds in transferring huge amounts of cash flow money to the moneyed class. The cash value of a $50,000 house becomes a cash flow value of around $250,000 transferred from the citizen who exchanges time and labor, mental and physical, for money, to the ones who had the money to buy the house outright, in cash, to start with. When the worker sells after the title is secured, they will be lucky to get $100,000. They are still out at least a $100,000 plus in straight cash.

25 Consider GDP as a crude measure of real wealth production. Suppose it increases at 4% a year. Suppose that at the same time, the interest rate runs at 5%. For a while, the production of real wealth can grow. The population increase, providing more workers, and the existing reserves of the scarce resources may be ample enough to pose no near term approach to the physical limit. The Earth is a very large bottle, but eventually we have the same reality and fate of the fruit fly.

But say for a hundred years, the rates hold up. The holder of production assets falls seriously behind the holder of money assets, principally because of the geometric advantage of adding each year's increase to the original base. When the child is admonished to save, it is to save money, not newspapers. The advantage of holding money as a substitute for real wealth, is a psychologically deep cultural wisdom. Even the dimwitted, over enough generations, can observe the truth. Holding money pays better than holding anything else.

26 The correlation between real wealth and money is strictly empirical. Without the concrete limit of real economic production, money in the abstract can increase through artificial mathematical contrivances, and can do so quite

separately from whatever is going on in real wealth production. This is why so many spasms of the geometric mismatch end up in speculations. Surely no one ever believed a tulip bulb was ever worth 10,000 guilders, except that a greater fool might be found to pay 10,500, expecting the price to go up indefinitely. But where did the greater fool get the money to begin with? Without excess in the money supply, speculation is brief and moderate.

The problem occurs when money is used disportionately as a substitute for real wealth. The maldistribution of real wealth is a necessary consequence. The possessor of a geometric increase can take that new quantity back into the market of real goods and exercise a significantly greater leverage in buying up real wealth.

Consider two individuals, both starting with $100,000 of assts. One holds these assets as a business which provides $50,000 a year for material consumption. The other holds the assets as money, returning 50%, $50,000 a year, also for available material consumption. One saves and reinvests to secure the $50,000 return. The other saves and reinvests, but this return is added to the base. Money does not degrade. It has has no inherent life cycle. In ten years, the holder of money will be in position to buy a greater proportion of the real wealth than his one time equal.

27 Another illustration of the geometric separation of money from the real wealth is afforded by the economy of the ditch digger world. Assume two ditch diggers, one who digs 10 shovelfuls and one who digs 12. Suppose 11 are needed to secure the base material necessaries. To make up the difference, the one borrows a shovelful from the other. Further suppose a rate of interest is imposed at one shovelful for each seven borrowed. At the end of a week, the one has produced 14 less shovelfuls, and owes 8 to the other. Obviously, by the end of the year, two who were nearly equal naturally to begin with, now have radically different proportions of the real wealth. To be sure, this is a bad contract, but it easily shows how very minor differences between individuals can become the difference between lord and serf, for the leverage of money interest effectively reduces the one, over the long run, to monetary bondage, where one's entire conceivable output for the rest of one's life is insufficient to repay the holder of the bond.

28 Natural differences in real wealth production create stable gaps between individuals within the population. For example, land varies in productive yield. One who farms bottomland fares better than one who farms hill country. A

hill country farmer may get 50 bushels per acre, while a bottomlands farmer may get a 100. Initially they stand in a 2:1 ratio of produced wealth. Further assume that it takes 40 bushels per acre to provide the basic material standard of living necessaries. One has a surplus of 10, the other 60. Thus far the inequality is based on natural differences. Clearly the difference grows. After 20 years, one has 200 to the other's 1,200, a gap in wealth of 1,000.

Now assume that the surpluses are converted to money and held. This is describable as an annuity of a future sum, a mathematical monetary device. Let the annuity run for 20 years at 10%. Now the one holds 572.75 to the other's 3436.50, a gap now of 2,863.75. A difference now exists, after 20 years, that would have taken 54 years if produced at the original differential rates of real wealth production. Thus the purchasing power of natural advantage is geometrically enhanced. With money, the rich can get richer, and the poor poorer, for the increase enables the one to buy out the other.

The divergent mathematical natures of real wealth and money are clearly evident, and the consequences on the artificial maldistribution of wealth objectively demonstrable.

29   The cumulative distribution of wealth in most civilizations long employing money as a substitute for real wealth show an increasing maldistribution of the same. What is striking is the pertinacity of the privileged and fortunate to not only preserve their extra measures as a divine right, but to also spend fortunes to influence the government to grant them even greater favors and expanded wealth. Indeed, they will subjugate and police where they can. This in spite of all the efforts of the great religions.

Such behavior is at war with natural human society. It denies common purpose, common rights, or any complaint of injustice or unfairness. By the fortune that the system has blessed them with, and, to be fair, by their efforts, the moneyed class buys themselves into the mansions of heaven while still living on this Earth with the rest of us. Their fortune is perfectly clear to them. They are better than we are. They divide the world into "our people" and the less advantaged others, so obviously inferior as to deserve their fate. As if two species of human exist, one superior and entitled, and the other degraded and dispossessed. This is the lingering shadow of feudalism and slavery still darkening the landscape of so called civilized society.

30 The work of Friedman and the monetarists confirm two key points. One, that real wealth production is an arithmetic phenomena while money creation is a geometric phenomenon. Therefore, the money supply must be accurately measured and tightly controlled so that its increases mimic arithmetic behavior, proportionally matching the increase in real wealth. In this, Friedman ranks with Malthus. Two, when despite careful control, the money supply undergoes a geometric expansion, serious distortions occur in economic activity, inflation, speculation, and in bankruptcies and forfeitures due to debt burden, which are again always a geometric draw against real wealth, when finally real wealth production sags once the drug of fabulously expanding money wears off, as it invariably does.

31 The distortions caused by money changing from a measure of wealth to a substitute for wealth, and thus managed independently, if at all, is itself painfully evident throughout the history of European banking. Once the bounties of geometrically expanding the money supply are tasted, the boom begins in earnest. Money is created by credit loans. Loans, carrying interest, compounded at intervals, exacts a geometric draw on the existing resources of wealth. The accelerating surplus of artificial, substitute wealth bids on real wealth, and by being leveraged, draws greater proportions of the real wealth to itself. Obviously someone must give up wealth resources to provide this windfall. They are called the have not's, the poor, and in disguise, most of the middle class.

But every so often, like fire burning down a house after warming it, the gap between real wealth and the artificial wealth of money becomes so wide as to snap. Money can vanish geometrically as well. In the collapse, many suffer. But the suffering is maldistributed, too. The fools who mistimed their monetary moves are punished. But the base is still money, often still slightly increased. The real fools are the rest of us. We still owe a cash flow geometrically expanded beyond the original principal in interest to somebody having the money to start with. Or lose what real wealth we have acquired on credit.

The so called economic corrections correct the common people far more definitively than they correct the well situated. Even in economic hard times, the gap between rich and poor grows larger.

32 In economic prosperity, the rich gain more than their less fortunate fellow citizens, the common majority who spend the lion's share of their wealth on what are counted as necessaries. This fortune grants them, given the geometric properties of money. They presume merit and intrinsic worth over the common, but that is their Freudian delusion. One simply cannot admit the unwashed to the dinner party.

In economic depression, the rich lose less ground than the common masses. In terms of Maslow's hierarchy of human needs, the general welfare of the people being the base social political need, the many give up security and dignity needs just to keep eating and maintaining a hovel, while the rich give up self actualization for the droll and dreary purgatory of country club life

A loss of half one's income or present wealth for many means loss of house and car, as well as a serious and traumatic degradation in the basic necessaries of material existence. When the flow of wealth coming to you far exceeds this base standard, you can lose half and still eat steak.

33 One cause for this increasing maldistribution during hard times is due to a Maslow like hierarchy of uses for wealth. There is an enormous psychological difference between a citizen spending all for necessities, and then losing ground, and the well to do, who can retrench, only truly injuring their egos, still covering necessities easily, and still having discretionary income. This is the difference between forgoing cable television and forgoing the summer on the Riviera. When basic heating costs go up 200%, the common must give up the cell phone or dinners out, while the well to do give up lobster and the gardener.

34 Everyone sees the maldistribution of real wealth, as well as its increasing maldistribution, in many present national economies. The gap between rich and poor in the United States is embarrassing for a society supposedly committed to eradicating organized privilege and favor. But in other countries the gap passes beyond shame to evil. The benefactors of the geometric distortion, loosely called the rich and powerful, see little reason to change the present state of affairs, or even deign to address the problem. And they seem less restrained, more, ruthless, in destroying any threats to the sanctity of their bounty.

Some of us are moved by simple brute selfishness, adorned with a myth of superiority or divine blessing. Some apply self interest, striving to be rational, but simply cannot include all the variables needed to make a decent shot at the truth. Some see the hypocrisy, but still use the incredible complexity of the matter to obfuscate the essential immoral result. Some consider the system that rewards them so handsomely as handed down from Mt. Sinai, and immutable. You must become poorer so that I can become richer. Almost as if they are obliged to horde their benefit by some divine right of property, and to save you from the sin they are so amply allowed to indulge in themselves. How many robber barons got nicely boozed at night expounding upon their virtue in keeping worker wages as low as possible to save their souls from boozing it up in pubs.

All such attitudes are self serving, morally bankrupt, and blind to the commonweal, to the common sense sense of justice found in every naturally born human.

35 That increasing maldistribution of real wealth is a characteristic of marvelously affluent societies is the basest shame and the final arbitrary horror of so called advanced civilizations. None have succeeded in keeping the merely natural inequality within the distribution of real wealth stable. All have made the rich richer, and the poor poorer.

36 If, at the macroeconomic level, the problems caused by the incompatible quantitative natures of real wealth and money have been identified, and managed, for the sake of argument, reasonably well, the question becomes, what are the specific causes of wealth maldistribution? Why does the interior micro structure of wealth distort when the macro proportions between money and real wealth hold stable?

Two culprits are readily identifiable. One, if one holds money as a substitute for real wealth, and uses it to create money, employing the present theory of interest, which adds regular increases to the base, then those so positioned will experience a geometric expansion relative to the holders of real wealth, even if only slightly. Over the long run, this insures a serious, increasing maldistribution of real wealth at the micro level. Simply compare the fate of the mortgage holder with the payee who loses their job after ten years, and subsequently are foreclosed. The payee loses in real wealth space and time. They are dispossessed and on the street. The mortgage has already recovered the principal plus a lot of interest, and the "victim" of the default still holds title to the property, which still has some plausible market value. The hardship of the one is matched by the life breaking disaster of the other.

The overall, macro level of money may be controllable in theory, but the individual holders of debt may still enjoy the geometric lift and increasing leverage with respect to real wealth compared to those who hold most of their wealth as material things, real wealth. This is why the phrases, "land poor" or "working poor" have meaning.

The second cause of maldistribution is the so called fair "percentage increase" commonly found in government and corporate bureaucracies. Start two people at 10 and 20 thousand, and give each a so called fair 10% increase for 20 years. Because the increase is added to the base, the "apparent" real wealth gap between the two more than doubles. Yet once the difference in "value" was thought to be only $10,000. Did the one become twice as productive? Was the original value judgment flawed?

37 One usually thinks of the old Roman Catholic prohibition against usury, one of the dogmas overthrown by the Protestant Reformation, as some misguided idea trying to promote an economic brotherhood, matching the alleged spiritual and moral brotherhood of human society. But what if it was also the influence of some primeval economist with a penetrating insight into the arithmetic nature of real wealth and the distorting effect of allowing a geometric phenomena, money, serve as a medium of exchange, thus artificially affecting the distribution of real wealth, thereby distorting and maldistributing it.

38 So the question becomes, are there any workable cures for the artificial enlargement of wealth, and its maldistributive malignancy this side of doomsday? The great religions have manifestly failed. Two even especially forbid usury in any form as a cardinal sin, Islam and Old Catholicism. Both have succumbed to the potent allure and powerful addiction that geometrically expanded wealth offers. Laws prohibit interest rates above 20 some percentage points, but all that does is somewhat lengthen the time needed to grossly fatten up one's share of the wealth. Instead of a few years, perhaps a generation is needed before the geometric magnitude of the effects are felt. And in time, bringing the injustice down fully on the third and fourth generation of those left behind.

39 We do not want to get rid of interest. The need for a return on investment, even as debt, is a psychological necessity. Ridding ourselves of interest is no more viable than pretending a perfectly equal distribution of wealth is

possible, given human nature. The principal reason Smith won out over Marx is because Smith took real human nature in account, while Marx thought it could be instantly conditioned into some ideal beyond its capacity to change. Forced, perfect equality is as unnatural as the warped maldistribution always found increasing in urbanized, civilized, so called capitalistic economies.

40 We need capital formation. Industrial production requires it, and we like the goods industrial production provides for our material standard of living. Our destiny in space requires it. We also want time based credit. We want citizens to own their own homes. All of them. For this, a return on investment is necessary.

What is needed is a new, more developed mathematical theory of interest, one that adds a progressive, logarithmic correction at the second moment for each increase in the first moment, the interest rate. The same problem facing Newton when he invented calculus to solve his descriptive problem of gravity mathematically. What the progressive income tax structure provides.

The same mathematical apparatus could also then be applied to replace the "percentage increase" cause of increasingly maldistributed wealth.

That is, micro controls as powerful as the macro controls are needed.

41 Another decisive strategy, again wholly impractical, would be to somehow regularly set the interest rate at some trigger statistic of real wealth production. But if set below, instead of above, the rate of increase of real wealth production. Instead of suffering the excesses of speculation, the geometric expansion of wealth beyond sustainable rates of real wealth productivity, the society would only occasionally experience mild flounderings while money supply caught up with real wealth. In the interim, the moneyed class would move closer to the working class.

But this is a theoretical curiosity only. Without a persuasive theory and ample evidence, no policy will ever reflect this strategy.

42 There once was a steep progressive structure to the income tax. A progressive structure is essentially a logarithmic correction to geometric expansion, however imprecise. Perhaps the past progressive correction was too steep. Pending a new theory of interest, we cannot know for sure. But after the

reactionary counterstroke so lauded in the Reagan administration, the tax on huge incomes has become flat, even after the Clinton bubble on upper middle class incomes. One wonders why the millionaires think it fair that they pay essentially the same percentage as the billionaires, so much their disadvantage.

43 The steeply progressive income tax was relict of the healthy, robust 50's, when the sheer solidarity created by the impossible war effort made the nation beat tribally for one season. But the inevitable maldistribution due to geometric expansion crept in, year by year, generation by generation, until the ground we have lost, in these most affluent times of human history, is a shame, an embarrassment, an open wound, and perhaps the best evidence of original sin in modern times.

Palaces arise amidst the hovels. Who benefits from this astounding state of affairs? Perhaps such a bloodless coup shows our apparent improvement over feudalism, when tens of thousands were hung or beheaded when the empowered, unnatural wealth holding classes, the aristocracy, the descendants of the last conquerors subjugating of the common people, came out of the fastness of their castle keeps, when the serfs and peasants needed to disperse to bring in the harvest, during the Peasant's Rebellion in Germany, after Luther, and enfired by Luther, and abandoned and repudiated by Luther. Such improvement in merely five hundred years.

44 Another impossible cure is to set limits on the margin of wealth. In nomadic, tribal society, such a limit was controlled by the physical limits of transportation and public inspection. In early agrarian society, the common living vicinity allowed public inspection again to work as a brake against the unnatural accumulation of wealth. But when human ingenuity produces surpluses, wealth must be measured. Rough rules of thumb do not do. So money is created to measure wealth. But the measure, money, becomes a thing in itself, and so the distribution of wealth is accordingly corrupted by the geometrical mathematical properties of money scale, unencumbered the restrictions of real wealth production.

Theodore Roosevelt, in his Autobiography, asked his fellow privileged peers, that once that they had all their improvements to existing property, and had added all that they had thought of, what more could they need? There is a limit of individual wealth. Wealth beyond that should be distributed by religious potlatches.

Opposing such ideal wishing is the prevalent, though largely subconscious, belief in the divine right of property.

45 There is no merit in money, only the advantage of possession.

0-595-31821-5